Here you may see the best portrait that,
later, I was able to make of him.

5 STEPS
ENGLISH

The Little Prince

낮은 단계부터 원문까지 한 권에 담은
단계 영어 어린 왕자

초 판 | 1쇄 2020 년 5월 4일
개정판 | 1쇄 2024 년 1월 10일

지 은 이 | 앙투안 마리 로제 드 생텍쥐페리
영어번역 | 스티브 오
정보맵핑 | 이야기 연구소
디 자 인 | 아름다운 다자인
감   수 | Michelle, Kim | HannahAllyse Kim | Kara-beth Carl | Edmund Nai
특허출원 | 10-2020-0012558
국제출원 | PCT/KR2020/002551

펴 낸 곳 | (주)도서출판동행
펴 낸 이 | 오승근
제 작 처 | 다온피앤피
출판등록 | 2020년 3월 20일 제2020-000005호
주   소 | 부산광역시 부산진구 동천로109, 9층
이 메 일 | withyou@withyoubooks.com
출판등록 | withyoubooks.com
카카오톡 | @동행출판사

단계별 요약정보 기술은 국내특허출원 및 PCT 국제출원을 받았습니다.

ISBN 979-11-91648-12-6
ISBN 979-11-91648-11-9 (세트)

낮은 단계부터 원문까지 한 권에 담은

단계 영어

어린왕자

등행

인터넷에서 사용되는 언어의 55.7%가 영어입니다. 인터넷 정보의 절반 이상이 영어로 되어있습니다. 영어 못하면 서러운 것은 인터넷에서도 마찬가지입니다. 그럼 한국어는 인터넷에서 어느 정도 차지할까요? 놀라지 마세요. 한국어는 1%도 안 되는 0.4%입니다. 영어로 정보를 해석할 수 있다는 것이 곧 55.7%의 정보를 다 접한다는 걸 의미하진 않습니다. 하지만 내가 할 수 있는데 안 하는 것과 처음부터 할 수 없는 것에는 분명 차이가 있습니다.

55.7% of the language used on the internet is English. English counts for more than half of the information on the internet. It would be sad if one is not proficient in English, not only in the real world but also on the internel. Then how much Korean occupies the language used on the internet? Do not be surprised. Korean occupies 0.4%, which is less than 1%. Being proficient in English does not always allow access to the 55.7% of the information. But there is a difference between things that I can do but I choose not to do, and things that I cannot do from the beginning.

영어에서 "말하기, 듣기, 읽기, 쓰기" 중 어느 하나 중요하지 않은 건 없습니다. 그러나 인터넷이 일상인 우리에게 더 필요한 것은 읽기라 생각합니다. 영어 읽기는 책을 읽듯이 영어로 그냥 읽는 것이 중요합니다. 하지만 그게 말처럼 쉽지 않습니다. 해보신 분들은 아시겠지만 어려운 단어들과 긴 문장들 때문에 책장이 넘어가질 않습니다. 사전 찾지 않고 모르는 단어를 유추해보려 해도 모르는 단어가 문장마다 나오는데 어떻게 유추할 수 있겠습니까?

"Speaking, listening, reading, and writing" are all important in using English. However, reading would be an essential skill, as surfing the internet is one of the daily routines in our lives. It is important to read in English as if you are reading a book. But It is not as it looks. For those who tried it, there are many difficult words and lengthy sentences, giving us a difficult time to flip to the next page. How could we not use dictionaries and instead use context clues if there are words that we do not know one after another?

어려운 영어 원문을 사전 없이도, 내용을 이해하며 읽을 수 있는 책이 단계별 영어 원서입니다. 한 번 아이들이 말을 배우는 과정을 생각해 보세요. '엄마', '아빠'와 같이 몇 안 되는 단어만 말하던 아이가 시간이 지나면 말이 길어지고 내용이 깊어집니다. 그러니까 처음엔 "엄마 밥 줘" 였는데, 시간이 지나면 "엄마 내가 좋아하는 김밥 먹고 싶어요" 처럼 표현에 깊이가 생긴다는 것이죠. 하지만 여기서 중요한 사실은, 표현은 달라졌지만 말하고자 하는 핵심 내용은 같다는 것입니다. 둘 다 "음식을 먹고 싶다(또는 배고프다)"라는 게 핵심입니다.

I Can Read English books help you to understand what you read without using a dictionary. Think of how babies learn a language. They only say a few words like 'mom' and 'dad,' but after a while, they learn how to mix the words to make sentences. If a child only knew how to say, "Mom, I want some food," he could express more comprehensively as time passes, saying for example, "Mom, I want to eat my favorite menu, Gimbap." The important thing here is that the child expressed his thoughts differently, but the message was the same. Both deliver a message that the child "wants to eat food(or he is hungry)."

단계 영어의 구성은 마치 아이들이 3~4년에 걸쳐서 언어가 성장하는 과정을 레벨1~5에 넣은 것과 같습니다. 레벨1이 4살 아이의 표현이라면, 레벨2 는 5살

아이의 표현이라 볼 수 있습니다. 전달하고자 하는 핵심 내용은 원문과 같지만, 그것을 표현하는 방식이 레벨에 따라 달라진다는 것입니다.

The 5 Steps English Books considered the different stages of language learning in children in a span of 3~4 years in levels one to five. If Level 1 corresponds to a four-year-old child's expressions, Level 2 corresponds to a five-year-old child's expressions. The message is the same, but how you express it would be different for each level.

레벨1은 가장 쉬운 어휘를 사용해서 문장을 짧게 만들었습니다. 레벨1을 읽고 이해할 수 있다면, 레벨2는 사전 없이도 충분히 내용을 유추하며 읽을 수 있습니다. 이게 가능하냐고요? 가능합니다. 인터넷에 넘치는 독자 후기가 이를 증명해주고 있습니다.

Level 1 is composed of short sentences with simple vocabulary. If you can understand what you read in the Level 1 book, you could use context clues to understand what you read in the Level 2 book without using a dictionary. Is this really possible? Yes, it is possible. Hundreds of customer testimonials on the internet prove this.

다시 한번 말씀드리지만, 책은 '읽어야' 합니다. 편안한 마음으로 읽어 보세요. 해석이 틀려도 괜찮고, 오해가 생겨도 괜찮습니다. 정확한 해석을 찾는 일에 집중하지 마시고 그냥 읽어 보세요. 성인도 모국어를 틀리게 사용할 때가 있지 않습니까? 그러니 틀리는 것을 겁내지 마시고 그냥 한 번 읽어 보세요.

We would like to emphasize again that a book should be "READ." Read the book comfortably. It is fine even if you interpret the content incorrectly and even if you misunderstand the messages. Do not focus on making correct interpretations, but just read. Even adults make mistakes when they speak in their mother language. Do not be afraid of making mistakes and just try to read the book.

사실 아이들은 모국어를 틀리면서 배워갑니다. 발음도 틀리고, 어순도 틀리고, 잘못된 단어도 사용하지요. 하지만 끊임없이 사용하기에 틀린 것을 고쳐 가면서 결국엔 올바른 언어로 사용하게 됩니다. 이렇듯 언어는 지속성이 중요합니다. 단계별 영어 원서는 특별한 준비작업 없이도 가볍게 책장을 열어 읽을 수 있기에 언어의 지속성을 가능하게 해주는 최적에 읽기 도구입니다. 지금 바로 레벨1을 읽어 보세요. "세상 모든 영어가 레벨1이면 좋겠어요."라고 하셨던 한 독자분의 고백을 여러분도 하시게 될 겁니다.

Even children learn their mother language from their mistakes. They make mistakes in pronunciation and word orders and sometimes use inappropriate words. But they never stop using the language and they correct their mistakes as they go until they can speak properly. Like this, sustainability is important in learning a language. I Can Read English Books are the best tools to learn a language in a sustainable manner as they do not require any special preparation. You can immediately start reading them. Start reading our Level 1 book. You will understand what our customer meant when she made a testimonial saying, "I hope all English in this world is Level 1."

자, 그럼 이제 시작해 보세요!

Now, it's your time to start reading!

Steve Oh

본 도서는 와디즈 크라우드펀딩을 통해 먼저 나왔습니다.
도서를 구매하신 서포터들의 좋은 평가로 인해
도서 분야 1위와 평점 5.0이라는 기록을 세웠습니다.

아래는 서포터들이 올린 실제 후기입니다.

wadiz
도서분야
1위

정말로 읽는 게 되네요. 세상 모든 영어가 1단계 레벨이었으면 좋겠네요. It is so surprising that I actually understand what I read. I hope all English in this world is in Level 1 _소리 Sori

매우 매우 좋습니다! 해외에 10년 거주한 누나가 읽어도 정말 좋은 책이라고 하네요. 단계별로 수준에 맞추어 읽을 수 있게끔 만들었다는 게 가장 크다고 해요. Very, very satisfying! My sister, who lived abroad, told me that it is an excellent book. The biggest advantage of the book is the classification in different levels so that people can read based on their proficiency level. _Dean James

한 번도 원서를 완독 해본 적이 없었는데 덕분에 이번엔 완독할 수 있겠어요!! 좋은 책 감사합니다♡♡♡ I have never finished reading an English books, but I was able to finish this time!! Thank you for a very useful book♡♡♡ _익명의 서포터 Anonymous supporter

처음 훑어보고 천재이신 듯! 했네요^^ 단계별 학습이라는 것은 누구나 알고 있는 것이지만 그걸 실제 제대로 한 번에, 한 곳에 구현해 놓으셨다는 게 대단하신 듯해요. 알찬 구성, 친절한 안내 덕분에 그동안 무심했던 영어 공부에 다시 의욕이 샘솟네요. The author must be a genius! I just skimmed it once, and I could really tell how perfectly step-by-step learning is expressed in the book. Everyone knows what step-by-step learning is, but I have never seen such a perfect book. Thanks to the full of solid contents, and the well-designed guidelines of the book, I could start again enthusiastically studying English. _정숙임 Jungsook Lim

최고에요! 어떻게 이런 걸 만들 생각을 하셨는지... 다른 책들도 아주 많이 나왔면 좋겠어요 진짜! Outstanding! I wonder how they come up with such an idea... I hope there will be more series of these books published! For real! _김현주 Kim Hyunjoo

영어 공부에 많은 도움이 되고 있습니다. 영어 원서읽기 도전하시는 분들에게 추천해 드립니다. ^^ This book is so helpful in my English studies. I recommend this book to those who are trying to read English book:) _김현태 Kim Hyuntae

영어리딩에 단계별로 단어나 구문에 차이를 두어 좀 더 쉽게 다가갈 수 있고 단계별로 비교도 가능해서 영어 익히기에 좀 더 수월합니다. Vocabulary and sentence structure are different for each level to make reading in English easier. You can also compare the sentences of each level, which helps you learn English better. _익명의 서포터 Anonymous supporter

오늘 책 잘 받았습니다. 정말 엄청나게 노력하신 흔적이 보입니다. 오리지널 버전 직전까지 단숨에 다 읽었는데, 선물용으로도 손색이 없을 것 같습니다. Received the book well today. The effort put into this book is clearly evident. I finished reading until the previous level of the original book. They would be a good gift for those who need them. _이장호 Lee Jangho

아직 1단계지만 원서를 읽을 수 있다는 게 신기합니다. 작은 성공으로 자신감을 얻어서 더 열심히 할 수 있을 것 같아요! 다음 시리즈도 기다리고 있습니다. I am still reading Level 1, but it is so fascinating that I could read an English book. A small success gave me confidence, and I could do much better! I am looking forward to the next series of books. _익명의 서포터 Anonymous supporter

영어로 된 책 한 권을 완독할 수 있다는 자신감이 생기네요!
I gained confidence after completely reading an English book!
_엘리 Elly

레벨1 다 읽었습니다. 정말 잘 만드셨다는 걸 새삼 느꼈습니다.
I finished reading Level 1. This book is really well-made.
_박명주 Park Myungjoo

학원에서 영어 가르치는 친구가 구성이 좋다고 하더라구요. 열심히 공부하겠습니다. My friend, who is teaching English in an academy, told me the contents are great. I will do my best to study English.
_단호박 Sweet Pumpkin

감사합니다~ 책 잘 읽고 있습니다. 원서 쉽게 읽는 재미가 쏠쏠하네요. Thank you! I am enjoying this book. It is so fun reading an English book. _솔이 Soli

책이 너무 훌륭하고, 요즘 원서를 읽는 감동을 느끼고 있습니다. This book is really outstanding, and I am experiencing how great it is to read an English book. _Kim Gwang Sung

10살 된 딸아이가 큰 흥미를 갖고 읽고 있습니다. 감사합니다. 이 기회에 영어를 읽는 재미를 느꼈으면 좋겠네요. My ten-year-old daughter is having fun reading this book. Thank you! I hope she will gain interest in reading English books. _하철은 Ha Cheoleun

표지도 아주 예쁘고 도입부터 부담스럽지 않은 레벨로 읽으니 지루하지 않고 재밌게 읽을 수 있습니다! The cover is cute, and the opening chapters are written at an easy level. It is not boring and fun to read! _배윤경 Bae Yoonkyung

아이들에게 읽어주고 있어요. 영어에 자신 없는 초등5 아들은 Level 1,2를 읽어주니 재밌게 듣고, 영어 잘하는 중2 딸은 Level 1~5를 한 챕터 단위로 읽어주니 흥미로워합니다. I am reading a book for my kids. My 5th-grade son, who is not confident in English, is having fun when I read Levels 1 and 2. While my daughter, who is in her second year of middle school and good at English, is fascinated as I read chapters for all five levels. _김라미 Kim Lamy

어린왕자를 어렵지 않게 읽을 수 있어서 좋았어요. 영어책을 보면 거부감이 드는데 아기자기하고 레벨별로 구분되어 있어서 영어 초보에게도 부담감이 덜 드네요. 책도 깔끔하고 이뻐서 선물용으로도 좋아요. It was good to read The Little Prince in English easily. I had a hard time reading English books, but the books are charmingly decorated, and the step-by-step levels of the books are really good for beginners. The covers of the books are neat and cute. It can be given away as a gift. _디디야 Didiya

몇 챕터 읽어 봤는데 와디즈에서 펀딩한 것 중에 가장 만족스럽습니다. 영어를 잘하는 편도 아닌데 진짜 잘 읽히네요. 노인과 바다도 나오면 꼭 펀딩할게요. I just read some chapters, and it was the most satisfying project I have funded in Wadiz. I could read it very well even if I am not good at English. I will surely fund another project if you publish The Old Man & The Sea. _시딘 Cidin

재미있게 읽고 있어요!! 전 챕터를 레벨 순서대로 하나씩 읽고 있어요. 원서로 읽을 때 어렵긴 해도 문장의 뜻을 알도 읽으니 아주 좋습니다!! I am having fun reading the books! I started reading from the lowest level, going up to the higher levels. Though it is hard to read an English book, it is readable as I know what the message is as I read the sentences. _백예지 Paek Yeji

이만한 단계별 영어 지침서가 또 있을까 싶네요. I wonder if there would be a better English guide aside from these _**익명의 서포터 Anonoymous supporter**

굿입니다. 내용과 디자인 모두 만족합니다. 이 책을 만들기 위해 열심히 노력한 저자의 노력이 눈에 보이는 듯 하네요. So good. I love the content and the design. It is evident that much effort has been made to make these books. _**배현학 Bae Hyunhak**

정성 가득한 게 느껴지는 책 잘 받았어요. 단계별로 읽을 수 있는 원서라는 아이디어도 너무 좋은데 상품도 너무 잘 만들어져서 감동입니다. Thank you for the books made with sincerity of the author. The idea of reading English books at different levels is so great, and the books are well-designed. _**익명의 서포터 Anonymous supporter**

단계별 원서 읽는 듯한 아주 재밌어요!차근차근 레벨 올리면서 영어에 흥미를 유발하네요! 차기작도 너무 기대됩니다..! It is so fun reading English books at different levels! A step-by-step approach makes English studying so fun! I am looking forward to the next books! _**김민찬 Kim Minchan**

책이 예뻐서 소장 가치도 높고 무엇보다도 끝까지 포기하지 않고 영어 원서를 읽을 수 있도록 제작한 부분이 마음에 듭니다:) The holding values of the books are high as the books are really cute. I also love how the books are designed to help readers not to give up on reading English books :) _**김지영 Kim Jiyoung**

제가 원서를 차근히 읽으면서 읽을 수 있다는 게 좋았고 다른 것도 기대하고 있습니다. It felt so good that I could read English books calmly and orderly. I am looking forward to the next books. _**김희선 Kim Heesun**

하나하나 제대로 의미를 파악해가며 원서를 읽고 싶어서 첫 도전을 와디즈에서 했어요. 생각보다 잘 만들어진 것 같아서 읽는 내내 재미 있네요. 다른 책들도 궁금합니다. I made my first step in reading English books while identifying the meaning of the words one by one by funding in Wadiz. The books are more well-designed than I expected, and reading is so much more fun. I am curious about the other books as well. _신설아 Shin Seola

아주 좋은 책입니다. 좋아하는 책을 여러 단계로 보니 영어 공부도 되고 재미도 있고요~~ 다른 사람들에게도 선물하고 싶은 마음이 들어 꼭!! 앵콜 펀딩해주셨으면 해요^^ These are great books. As my favorite book is divided into different levels, I could learn English much easier, and it is fun reading them~~ I would like to give them as gifts to my friends!! I hope there will be an encore deal soon :) _임원규 Lim Wongyu

뒤로 갈수록 어찌 될지는 모르겠지만 우선 낮은 레벨부터 쉽게 읽히니 자신감이 생깁니다^^ I am not sure how I would feel in the latter levels. But for the lower levels, I gained confidence as the books could be read easily :) _익명의 서포터 Anonymous supporter

일단 계속 읽고 외우고 반복 학습 하려고 노력 중입니다. 이런 분류의 책이 많이 나오면 더 좋을 것 같습니다. I am trying to read continuously, memorize words, and repeat reading them. I hope there will be more books like these _Anphaca

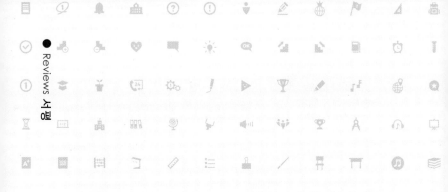

제가 영어원서를 읽는 날이 올 줄 몰랐습니다. 매일 영어 공부를 다짐하지만, 기초단어밖에 공부하지 못하고 야속하게 세월이 흘러 주부가 되었네요. 주부가 되어도 놓지 못했던 영어라는 큰마음의 짐이 이 책을 접하면서 마음의 짐이 아닌 마음의 양식이 되었습니다. 한 단어, 한 줄, 한 페이지를 넘길 때마다 어렵던 영어가 읽히는 재미에 시간 흐르는 줄도 몰랐습니다. 이젠 아이들에게 영어원서를 읽어주며 함께 이야기를 나눌 수 있게 되었습니다. 정말 「단계 영어」에 감사드릴 뿐입니다.

_황혜미

I never imagined that a day would come when I could read English books. I always thought of studying English, but I turned old and am now a housewife. I only learned the basics until now. After becoming a housewife, I always thought of studying English, and I had a burden on my mind. I have disburdened my mind after reading the books and these books are now my mental food. As I turned the pages, it was so fun reading one word after the other. It was so fun that I was not aware the time went so quickly. Now, I am reading books to my children and having fun discussions. Now, "5 Steps English," and I really appreciate it.

_Hwang Hyemi

처음에는 제가 과연 독파할 수 있을까? 하는 생각이 들었습니다. 항상 다른 것도 읽다가 도중에 포기했으니까요... 하지만 이 책은 딱 읽는 순간... 와~ 이번에는 진짜 내가 다 읽을 수 있겠구나! 이번에는 책장에 장식품이 되지 않겠구나! 그런 생각이 들었습니다. 지금도 계속 제 손에는 이 책이 있네요^^ 저처럼 도중에 포기했던 경험이 있으신 분들이라면 이 책을 강력히 추천합니다. 다른 분들도 저처럼 같은 경험을 하시기를 바랍니다.

_강민지

At first, I questioned if I could finish reading them. I always gave up reading other books. But as soon as I read this book, I thought that I could finish reading it! I had a strong feeling that it would no more be a decoration on my shelf! As I write this testimonial, I am holding this book :) For those who gave up reading English books just like me, I strongly recommend you these books. I hope others will have the same experience as I had.

_Kang Minji

진작에 이런 책이 나왔더라면, 난 영어를 포기하지 않았을 것이다.

1레벨은 낯설었지만,

2레벨에서 두려움이 사라지고,

3레벨부터 자신감이 생기자,

4레벨이 읽고 싶어졌으며,

5레벨을 읽으면서 비로소 원서에 길들었다.

원서를 읽고 싶다면 읽고 싶은 책을 찾지 말고, 읽을 수 있는 책을 찾아라.

그게 바로 이 책이다.

_이윤민

I would not have given up studying English if there were books like these in the past.

It was a little awkward when I read Level 1,

but I overcame the fear as I read Level 2,

gained confidence in Level 3,

had a strong desire to read Level 4,

and I adapted to reading English books as I read Level 5.

If you want to read an English book, do not search for what you want.

Search for a book that you can read.

And these are books that you can read.

_Lee Yoonmin

혹시 이 책이 영어 초보자들만을 위한 책이라고 생각했다면 정말 잘못 봤다. 이 책은 영어 초보들에게 세세한 단어를 단계별로 알아가는 재미를 줄 수 있고, 동시에 한국 주입식 영어교육에서 살아남았지만 스피킹이 서투른 소위 중급자들에게는 점점 쉽게 말하는 방법을 알려주고 있는 책이다. 이 책은 최소 2번은 읽어야 한다. 단계별로 올라갔다가 다시 내려오면서 당신의 영어 실력은 향상될 것이라고 장담한다. 특히 중급자들은 분명히 느낄 수 있을 것이다. 어떠한 단어를 몰라도 대신 훨씬 쉬운 단어로 말할 수 있음을, 발음이 틀려도 상관없고 소리가 작아도 상관없으니 꼭 입으로 소리내 읽기를 바란다.

_여운호 (쿠노잉글리쉬 대표)

If you thought the books were only for the English beginners, then you are wrong. These books give fun to beginners by letting the readers know the meaning of the words on a step-by-step basis. At the same time, they teach the intermediate learners, who are victims of cramming education, how to speak English easily. The books should be read at least twice. If you read the books one by one, going up and down the levels, you could feel your English skills are improved. I am sure that intermediate learners would relate to what I am saying. Even if you do not know what to say, you will learn how to say it in easy words. It does not matter if you pronounced it wrongly. I recommend you to read it with your mouth, even in a small voice.

_Yeo Woonho (CEO of Cuno English)

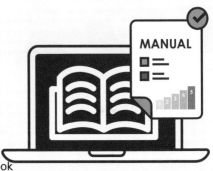

바람직한 도서 사용법
Tips on reading the book

이 책의 목적은 여러분이 '영어 원서를 사전 없이 읽도록 돕는 것'입니다. 사전을 찾거나 문법을 생각하며 읽으시면 안됩니다. 레벨 1~3은 현대 영문법을 바탕으로 제작했지만, 레벨 4, 5는 1943년 초판본의 영문 스타일을 존중했습니다. 레벨 5에 나오는 다소 어색한 고전 문학 표현은 하급 레벨을 통해 충분히 이해하실 수 있습니다.

The purpose of our books is for you to 'read English books without using a dictionary.' Do not search for a word in the dictionary or do not think of the grammar. Levels 1 to 3 are made based on modern English grammar, but Levels 4 and 5 preserve the English style of the original book. Awkward expressions found in Level 5 can be understood after reading the lower level books.

일반적으로 한글로 쓰인 책을 우리가 어떻게 읽는지 생각해 봅시다. 대부분 국어사전을 옆에 두고 읽지는 않습니다. 모르는 단어가 나오면, 유추해보거나 그냥 넘어갑니다. 단어 하나 때문에 내용이 이해되지 않을 때, 비로소 사전을 찾습니다.

Think about how we read Korean books in general. We do not use a dictionary while reading books. We try to infer the meaning or pass by a word that we do not know. We only use a dictionary when we cannot comprehend a sentence due to a single word.

영어도 이런 방식으로 읽는다면, 영어에 대한 두려움을 없애고 높기만 하던 영어 장벽을 허물 수 있습니다. 공부하는 게 아니라, 좋은 고전을 읽는다는 생각으로 책장을 넘겨보세요. 그렇게 레벨 1, 2를 읽었다면, 레벨 3도 큰 부담 없이 읽을 수 있습니다. 우리의 뇌는 생각보다 똑똑합니다. 같은 내용을 두 번 보고 이를 바탕으로 조금 추가된 내용을 읽으면, 모르는 부분도 쉽게 유추할 수 있습니다.

If you read English books in the same way, you can overcome fear and break down the barriers to reading English books. You are not studying; rather you are just reading a book. If you have read Levels 1 and 2, you could easily understand what you read in the Level 3 book. Our brain is smarter than we think. If we read something repeatedly and if we encounter some additions to it, we can easily infer when we read something unfamiliar.

레벨 4, 5는 영어 기초 값에 따라 읽는 속도가 다를 겁니다. 읽는 속도가 모르는 단어 때문에 느리다면, 딥러닝 단어장의 도움을 받아보시기를 권장합니다.『I Can Read The Little Prince, 딥러닝 어린 왕자 단어장』을 활용해 영어 단어의 뜻을 유추해보세요. 영어사전에서 단편적인 뜻만 확인하고 읽으면, 뜻을 금세 잊어버립니다. 하지만 딥러닝 단어장의 인접어로 내가 모르는 단어의 뜻을 미루어 추측한다면, 기억에 오래 남을 수 있습니다. 반면, 읽는 속도가 문장해석의 문제라면, 영어 독해에 일정 시간을 투자해야 합니다. 낮은 레벨의 문장들을 여러 번 읽은 후에 레벨 4나 5에 도전하는 게 좋습니다.

The reading speed when you read Levels 4 and 5 will be different depending on your basic knowledge of English. If your reading speed is slow due to encountering words that you do not know, we recommend you use the Deep Learning Vocabulary. Try to infer the meaning of the words through the 『I CanRead The Little Prince, Deep Learning Vocabulary』. If you search for a word in a dictionary, you will easily forget the word's meaning. But if you try to infer the meaning of the words by looking at the words adjacent to the words that you do not know through the Deep Learning Vocabulary, it will not be easily forgotten. However, if your reading speed is slow due to interpreting the sentences, you have to invest some time in reading. Try to read the sentences in the books in the lower levels several times before reading the Level 4 and 5 books.

다시 한번 말씀드리지만, 책은 '읽어야' 합니다. 편안한 마음으로 읽어 보세요. 해석이 틀려도 괜찮습니다. 오해가 생겨도 괜찮습니다. 우리는 지금까지 그렇게 실수를 하며 언어를 배워왔습니다. 정확한 해석을 찾는 일에 집중하지 맙시다. 다 큰 어른도 모국어를 사용할 때 실수합니다. 실수를 바탕으로 끊임없이 수정하며, 사용하고 있는 것이지요.

We would like to stress this out again: books are to be 'read'. Read the books comfortably. It is fine even if you interpret the sentences incorrectly or if you misunderstand the meanings. We have made mistakes when we learn our own language. Do not focus on making perfect interpretations. Even adults make mistakes when using their own language. Mistakes are corrected as they speak the language.

틀릴지라도 많이 사용해야 합니다. 어린아이는 모국어를 말하면서 수없이 틀립니다. 발음도 틀리고, 어순도 틀리고, 읽는 것도 틀립니다. 하지만 끊임없이 사용해 올바른 언어로 확립해 갑니다. 다양한 정보를 계속 접해야 내가 잘못 알고 있는 내용을 고칠 수 있습니다.

Even if you get it wrong, you have to repeat it many times. Kids make many mistakes when they speak their language. They make mistakes in word orders, and they are not good at reading. But as they speak endlessly, they learn how to speak correctly. It is important to be exposed to any information to correct your mistakes.

그러기에 지속해서 책을 읽는 게 중요합니다. 잘못 알고 있는 문장을 제대로 해석하려고 많은 시간을 쏟기보단, 그 시간에 한 문장이라도 더 읽는 것이 낫습니다. 많이 읽다 보면 어려웠던 문장, 잘못 이해했던 문장도 자연스럽게 고쳐집니다.

Therefore, it is important to read continuously. It is better to read one more sentence rather than spend time interpreting a sentence that you cannot understand. If you read many times, you will eventually learn the true meaning, and you will be able to read difficult sentences.

단계 영어 『어린 왕자』는
영어 독해가 어려운 분들을 위해 만들어진
단계별 영어원서입니다.
5 Steps English 『The Little Prince』
is divided into several levels and
is made for those who are have
a difficult time reading English books.

책의 특징 Features of the books

01 높은 곳을 계단으로 한 걸음씩 오르는 것처럼, 어려운 영어 원문을 레벨에 따라 한 단계씩 읽을 수 있게 만든 책입니다. 레벨에 따라 차례대로 읽으면 어린 왕자 영어 원문도 사전 없이 자연스럽게 읽게 됩니다.

Just like climbing a high place with stairs, the books are made to read English books step-by-step on different levels. If you read one level at a time, you will eventually be able to read The Little Prince in English.

02 레벨 1부터 레벨 4까지의 어린 왕자 본문은 레벨 5인 어린 왕자 원문을 자연스럽게 읽을 수 있도록 단계별 정보설계 기술로 제작되었습니다.

Books, Levels 1 to 4 of The Little Prince are designed for you to be able to read the original version, which is Level 5.

03 원문의 중요 부분만 발췌 편집한 것이 아닌 원문을 논리적 단계로 요약해서 만들었기에 레벨별 문단 수와 챕터 수가 원문과 거의 동일합니다.

We did not modify the important parts of the original book. We logically summarized the book for each level. So the paragraphs and chapters of the books on the lower levels are almost similar to the original.

셀프 테스트 Self-evaluation

책장을 넘겨 레벨 1의 내용을 읽었을 때, '이 정도면 읽을 수 있겠다.'는 생각이 든다면 이 책은 당신에게 맞는 책입니다.

If you read the first page of Level 1 and thought, "I could read this book," then the book is appropriate for you.

단계별 특징 Features for each level

LEVEL 1

구 성
Com-
ponents
원문 내용의 핵심을 가장 쉬운 단어와 문장으로 재구성하고 현재시제 동사를 사용했습니다.
Original words are replaced with simple words, restructured sentences, and used present verb tenses.

효 과
Benefits
영어 자신감 향상! Gain confidence in English!
원문 정보를 표현할 수 있는 쉬운(필수) 단어와 문장이 당신의 영어 자신감을 한 층 성장시킬 것입니다.
Simple(Essential) words and restructured sentences that express the original book in simplicity will help you gain confidence to another level.

빠른 도서 내용 파악 Quick interpretation of the content
원문의 핵심을 담았기에 전체 내용을 빠르게 이해할 수 있습니다.
Contains the key points of the story, making it easy to understand.

성취감 형성 Earn a sense of achievement
레벨 1은 짧고 쉽지만, 독립된 한 권의 책입니다. 레벨 1을 다 읽었다면 어린 왕자 영어 원서를 일독한 것입니다.
Level 1 is short and easy, but it is still a book. If you finished reading Level 1, then it means that you have read The Little Prince once.

LEVEL 2

구 성
Com-
ponents

레벨 1의 문장 구조에서 동사 시제를 원문과 비슷한 시제로 바꿨습니다.

Has a similar sentence structure to the Level 1 book, but the verb tenses are changed to similar tenses used in the original copy.

효 과
Benefits

동사 변화 파악 Identification of verb tenses

레벨 1과 비교해서 읽으면 동사 시제 변화를 자연스럽게 확인할 수 있습니다.

You can clearly see the difference in the verb tenses compared to Level 1.

독서 속도 향상! Increase reading speed!

이미 읽은 기본 영어 문장 구조가 있기에 레벨 1보다 빠른 속도의 읽기가 가능합니다.

As you have already read Level 1 and know the sentence structures, you can read it faster.

LEVEL 3

구 성
Com-
ponents

핵심 정보에 추가되는 내용과 레벨 2보다 한 단계 높은 단어와 문장으로 되어 있습니다.

Uses more complicated words and sentence structures than the Level 2 book, and a few more key points of the story are added.

효 과
Benefits

자연스러운 단어 유추
Infer the meaning of the words naturally

레벨 1, 2를 통해 기본 단어와 문장 구조가 파악되어 한 단계 높아진 단어와 추가된 문장들도 쉽게 유추하며 읽을 수 있습니다.

As you have read the Levels 1 and 2 books, the basic words and sentence structures will be familiar. Thus, the meanings of the words and sentences added can be inferred as you read.

LEVEL 4

구 성
Com-
ponents
레벨 5인 원문을 자연스럽게 읽을 수 있게 만들어 놓은 단계입니다.
This level is designed to help readers understand what they will read in the Level 5 book.

효 과
자기 신뢰 Self-trust
이미 어린 왕자를 세 번 읽은 당신에게 레벨 4는 어렵지 않게 읽을 수 있는 단계가 되었습니다.
As you have read The Little Prince three times, you will be able to read Level 4 easily.

독해능력 향상 Increase reading comprehension
레벨 5 원문을 자연스럽게 읽을 수 있게 도와줍니다.
Helps readers understand what they will read in the Level 5 book.

LEVEL 5

드디어 원문입니다. 난생처음 보는 단어들과 관용어들을 만나게 됩니다. 하지만 두려울 것이 없습니다. 당신에게는 레벨 4가 있습니다. 막히는 단어는 사전을 찾기 전 레벨4를 통해 유추해 보세요. 이렇게 상상하며 단어 뜻을 찾았을 때 그 단어는 오랫동안 당신의 기억 속에 자리 잡게 됩니다.

Finally, the original copy. You will be encountering new words and idioms. But there is no need to be afraid. You have the Level 4 book. Try to infer the meanings of the words with the help of the Level 4 book if you have no idea what the words mean. Imagining this way to learn the meaning of a word will last longer in your memories.

머리말 Preface   4

독자후기 Reviews   8

서평 Reviews   14

사용설명서 Manual   18

맺음말 Postscript   374

The Little Prince **LEVEL 1**

Chapter 1~5	**31~39**
Chapter 6~10	**40~47**
Chapter 11~15	**48~55**
Chapter 16~20	**56~61**
Chapter 21~25	**62~70**
Chapter 26~27	**71~76**

The Little Prince **LEVEL 2**

Chapter 1~5	**79~87**
Chapter 6~10	**88~96**
Chapter 11~15	**97~104**
Chapter 16~20	**105~109**
Chapter 21~25	**110~118**
Chapter 26~27	**119~122**

The Little Prince LEVEL 3

Chapter 1~3	125~131
Chapter 4~6	132~138
Chapter 7~9	139~146
Chapter 10~12	147~153
Chapter 13~15	154~163
Chapter 16~18	164~167
Chapter 19~21	168~174
Chapter 22~24	175~179
Chapter 25~27	180~190

The Little Prince LEVEL 4

Chapter 1~2	193~199
Chapter 3~4	200~205
Chapter 5~6	206~210
Chapter 7~8	211~218
Chapter 9~10	219~226
Chapter 11~12	227~229
Chapter 13~14	230~238
Chapter 15~16	239~244
Chapter 17~18	245~248
Chapter 19~20	249~251
Chapter 21~22	252~259
Chapter 23~24	260~263
Chapter 25~26	264~274
Chapter 27	275~276

The Little Prince **LEVEL 5**

Chapter 1	279
Chapter 2	282
Chapter 3	286
Chapter 4	289
Chapter 5	293
Chapter 6	297
Chapter 7	299
Chapter 8	303
Chapter 9	307
Chapter 10	310
Chapter 11	316
Chapter 12	318
Chapter 13	319
Chapter 14	324
Chapter 15	328
Chapter 16	333
Chapter 17	335
Chapter 18	338
Chapter 19	339
Chapter 20	340
Chapter 21	342
Chapter 22	350
Chapter 23	352
Chapter 24	353
Chapter 25	356
Chapter 26	361
Chapter 27	370

영문 어린 왕자를 가장 쉬운 단어와 문장으로 읽어 보세요.
문장의 99%가 현재 동사로 만들어져
동사 변화의 어려움 없이 글을 읽을 수 있습니다.
잃어버린 영어 자존심을 Level 1 단계에서 찾아 보세요.

Read The Little Prince in simple words and sentences.
99% of the sentences are structured with present verb tenses.
You could read without experiencing the changing tenses of the verbs.
Gain confidence in English with Level 1.

THE ORIGINAL TEXT

Something was broken in my engine. And as I had with me neither a mechanic nor any passengers, I set myself to attempt the difficult repairs all alone. It was a question of life or death for me: I had scarcely enough drinking water to last a week.

LEVEL 1

My plane doesn't work in the desert. And I am alone. Also, I only have water for a week.

The Little Prince
LEVEL 1 🔖

Chapter 1

I see a big snake in a book. The snake eats an animal.

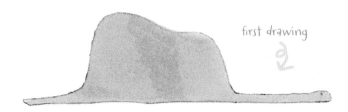

first drawing

After eating an animal, this snake does not need to eat for six months.

I draw that big snake. This is drawing number one.

But the man says, "This is a drawing of a hat."

My drawing is not of a hat. So, I draw an elephant inside

drawing No.2

the snake. This is drawing number two.

The man says to me, "Stop painting. Just do other things."
So, I give up being a painter.

Now I am a pilot. I can fly to many cities in the world.

I meet many great people. But, my mind does not change.

When I meet a smart person, I show them drawing number
one.

The person says, "That is a hat."

So, I never talk to that person about big snakes or the
jungle. I talk about card games and golf to make him
happy.

Chapter 2

I have only one friend, and he is the little prince.

My plane doesn't work in the desert. I am alone.
Also, I only have water for a week.

On the first night, I go to sleep on the sand. I hear a strange little voice in the morning.

"Draw me a sheep."
"What?"

There is a child who looks at me carefully. Here is a drawing of him. But, he looks sweeter than my drawing. That is because, as you know, I do not draw anymore.

I look at the child with surprise. You know that this is the desert. The child doesn't seem lost in the desert.

I say, "What are you doing here?"
And he repeats, "Draw me a sheep."

So I take out a sheet of paper and a pen. I am still in the desert.

As you know, I do not know how to draw. But, he says to me:

"That doesn't matter. Draw me a sheep..."
I do not draw a sheep. I draw the boa snake.

Then he says, "No, no! I do not want an elephant inside a boa snake. I need a sheep. Draw me a sheep."

So, I draw a sheep.
But he says to me, "No, this sheep is already very sickly."

So, I draw another one once more.
But, he says to me, "No."

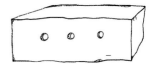

I draw another one in a hurry.
"This is a box. The sheep is inside the box."

He speaks with a bright face.
"That is exactly what I want. Does this sheep eat a lot?"
"Why?"
"In my place, everything is small."

I say, "He is a very small sheep. There is enough grass for him."
He says, "He's not that small. Look! He is sleeping.

Chapter 3

I get to know the little prince little by little.

When he sees my airplane, he asks, "What is that?"
"That is an airplane. It can fly."

He cries out, "What! You drop down from the sky?"
I answer softly, "Yes."
"Oh! That's funny! Ha ha!"

"So, you come from the sky too! Where is your star?"

I quickly ask him, surprised.
"Do you come from another star?"
But he does not answer.

He looks at the plane and says,
"You cannot come from very far
away."

After a time, he carefully takes the drawing of the sheep out of his pocket.

I ask many questions: "Where do you come from? Where do you want to take your sheep?"
He says, "This box is the sheep's house at night."

"If you are good, I can give you a rope to tie the sheep."
"Tie the sheep? That is strange."
"But if you don't tie the sheep, he goes away."
"It is okay because my star is so small.

Chapter 4

I have more information about the little prince. His star is about the size of a house.

When a star scientist finds a small star, he names it with a number. I believe the little prince came from star B-612.

A Turkish star scientist finds this star, but nobody believes him because he is wearing Turkish clothes.

A Turkish leader has great power. He orders his people to change from Turkish clothes to European clothes. The star scientist wears European clothes and talks about the B-612 again. Everybody believes his words.

I talk about numbers a lot because men like numbers. When you tell them that you have a new friend, they ask you these questions: "How old is he?" "How many brothers does he have?"

They always want to know numbers.

If you talk to men, you have to say, "I see a house that cost 20,000 dollars."

Then they say, "Oh, what a pretty house that is!"

If you say to them, "There is the little prince. He is lovely, and he is looking for a sheep."

They consider you to be like a child.

But if you say to them, "The star he comes from is B-612," they can understand what you say.

I like to begin this story like a fairy tale, but people may read it lightly and forget about it.

My friend is not with me. I don't want to forget the little prince, so I'm describing him here. This is why I buy a box of paints and pencils. But, it's not easy for me to draw again at my age.

Sometimes, I make some errors, but I try to draw as well as I can. I make mistakes on important details, but that is not my fault. My friend never explains anything to me.

Chapter 5

On the third day, I hear a story about the problem with the baobabs. (This is a tree name.)

The little prince asks me quickly, "Is it true that sheep eat little trees?"
"Yes, that is true."
"Ah! I am glad!"

"So, do they also eat baobab trees?" The little prince asks me again.
I say to him, "No, baobabs are not little trees. They are as big as castles."
But he wisely says, "Before they get so big, baobabs start out small."
"Yes, that's right."
"But why do you want the sheep to eat the little baobabs?"
"What are you talking about?"

He does not answer, so I have to find an answer myself. Maybe there is both good grass and bad grass on his star. If he sees bad grass, he has to pull it out fast. There are very bad seeds on the star. They are baobab seeds. If you wait too long to pull out the baobabs, they can split the small star into pieces.

The little prince tells me later, "You have to pull out baobabs just as you wash your face every day. It's boring, but it's easy."

One day he says to me, "Draw a picture and let the children know about this land. If you don't do it every day, you will have big problems."

So, I draw a star that is breaking from the baobab trees. "Children! Watch out for the baobabs!"

I draw that tree very carefully. I think this drawing is great.

I try to draw other pictures as well as I do the baobabs, but I can't. So, the other pictures are not as good as the picture of the baobabs.

The baobabs.

Chapter 6

Oh, little prince! Little by little, I understand your little and sad life.

On the fourth day, I learn more about the little prince. The little prince's star is so small that he can see the sunset at any time.

If he wants to see the sunset, he simply needs to move his chair a few steps forward.

The little prince says to me, "I can see the sunset 44 times!"

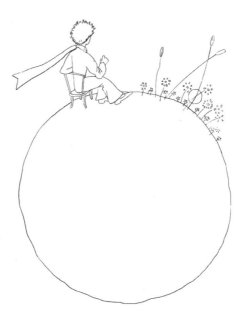

Chapter 7

On the fifth day, he suddenly asks me, "Does a sheep eat flowers, too?"

I answer him, "A sheep eats anything."

"A sheep eats roses?"

"Yes, sure."

"But roses have thorns that guard them. What use are thorns?"

I say what comes out of my mouth. "The thorns are no use at all."

"I don't believe you! Roses are weak, so they have thorns. They think that thorns are perfect weapons. Do you really believe that the flowers..."

I cry out, "No, no! I don't believe anything. Can't you see? I am very busy. I am fixing the plane. This is very important work for me."

He looks at me. "Important work? You talk just like the men! You mix everything up together..." He is very angry.

"I know a man. He does not love anyone. He only loves numbers. All day he says over and over, just like you, 'I am busy. I do important work.'"

"It is difficult for flowers to make thorns. But, do you think that is not important? Is the war between the sheep and the flowers not important?"

"There is only one flower in the world, but one little sheep can destroy it in a bite. You think that is not important!"

"If someone loves a flower, that flower is the only one in the world. He is happy just thinking about that flower. But, if the sheep eats that flower, he loses everything. You think that is not important!"

He cries with no sounds. I drop my tools. I take him in my arms. I say to him, "The flower that you love is not in danger. I can draw a mask for your sheep. I can..." I don't know what to say to him.

Chapter 8

On the little prince's star, the flowers are very simple. The flowers come out from the grass and go away peacefully.

One day, something comes out of the ground. It has small leaves. The little prince watches very closely over those small leaves.

The plant gets ready to make a flower. The flower prepares to show her beauty in her flower room. She carefully chooses her colors. She wants to come out when it is full of beautiful light. She is a very lovely plant.

The flower gets ready for a long time. Finally, she comes out. But, the flower says, "I am awake now. I don't look good." The little prince says to her, "Oh! How beautiful you are!" "Sure, I am."
"I think it's time to eat," the flower says. "Please think about my needs."
The little prince brings fresh water.

The flower says, "I am not afraid of tigers. I have four thorns." "Tigers don't eat plants," says the little prince.
"Well..." She changes her words. "I don't like the wind. I want you to put me under a glass cup. It is very cold here." She coughs two times. "The glass cup?"

The little prince loves the flower with all his heart. But he is unhappy because he thinks deeply about her words.

The little prince speaks his mind, "I do not listen to what she says. I just smell the flower. That's enough. But the truth is, I don't know how to understand her. I shouldn't have run away from her...

Chapter 9

The little prince cleans two volcanoes. After cleaning, he leaves his star. He cleans the third volcano. The third volcano doesn't work anymore. If you clean well, volcanoes are okay.

He removes the little baobabs. He waters the flower. He feels very close to tears.

"Goodbye," he says to the flower.
She doesn't answer.
At last, she says to him, "Forgive me and be happy... I love you too. I don't need the glass cup anymore."

"But the wind..."
"The cool night air is good for me. I am a flower."
"But the animals..."
"It's okay. Don't worry about that. Just go." She doesn't want him to see her crying.

He carefully cleaned out his active volcanoes.

Chapter 10

The little prince visits stars 325-330.

On the first star, there is a king. When the king sees the little prince, he says, "Ah! Here is a citizen."

Every man is a citizen of the king. The king calls to him, "Ah! Here is a citizen." And the king says, "Come closer to me."

The little prince wants to sit down, but he keeps standing because there is no place to sit.

The little prince yawns, but the king stops him.
"I'm sleepy, so I can't stop myself."
"Ah! Then I command you to yawn," the king says.
"Your command scares me... I can't."
"Then I... I command..." The king is a little bit angry because he has great power. So everyone must obey his commands.

He is a good king because he makes his commands understandable.
"May I sit down?" the little prince asks.
"I command you to do so," the king answers.

The little prince thinks to himself, "This star is so small."
"My lord," he says to the king, "over what do you rule?"
"Over everything," says the king.

"Over everything?" asks the little prince.

"Yes, over everything on every star," the king answers.

"The stars obey you?"

"Sure they do," the king says.

The little prince thinks, "What a great power." If he has that power, he does not need to move his chair to watch the sunset. He feels a bit sad. He remembers his star.

"I want to see the sunset," the little prince says.

"If I order a soldier to do an impossible command, who is wrong? the soldier or I?"

"You," says the little prince.

"That's right," the king says. "The command needs to be acceptable."

"What about my sunset?" the little prince asks.

"You can have your sunset, but you have to wait." The king answers.

"Until when?"

"Hmm, let me see. This evening, around twenty minutes to eight."

"I have nothing more to do here," he says to the king. "I will go on my way again."

"Do not go," says the king. "I can make you Minister of Law!"

"But there's no one here to judge!" the little prince says.

"Then you shall judge yourself," the king says to the little prince.

"But I can judge myself anywhere."

"Well then, you can judge the old mouse on our star. It's okay to give him the death penalty."

"I don't want to put anyone to death. I need to go on my way."

"No," says the king.

"If you command me to go, I can follow your command," the little prince says.

But the king has no answer. So the little prince goes on his way.

Chapter 11

A big talker lives on the second star. When he sees the little prince, he says, "Ah! Ah! You come to respect me."

"You wear a strange hat," says the little prince.
"This hat is for the welcome," he replies.

"Clap your hands," he says to the little prince. The little prince claps his hands. Then the man takes off his hat. The little prince and the big talker repeat these actions for five minutes.
"How can I make the hat fall to the ground?" the little prince asks.

The big talker only listen to good words. "Do you really respect me?" he asks.
"What does that mean, 'respect'?" the little prince asks.
"To respect means to believe 'You are the best at everything.'"

"But you are the only man on your star! Even if I respect you, what is the point? You are the only one." The little prince goes away.

Chapter 12

There is a drunk person on the third star. "What are you doing?" the little prince asks.

"I am drinking," he replies.
"Why are you drinking?"
"I want to forget."
"Forget what?" the little prince asks.
"Forget that I feel bad," he says.
"Feel bad about what?"
"Feel bad about drinking!" he answers.

"Men are very, very strange." The little prince goes away.

Chapter 13

There is a businessman on the fourth star. "Good morning," the little prince says to him. He doesn't answer.

"Three and two make five. Good morning. Fifteen and seven make twenty-two. Phew! That makes five-hundred-and-one million..."

"Five hundred million of what?" asks the little prince.
"Eh? Are you still there? I do very important work."
"Five hundred million of what?" asks the little prince again.

"I have three bad stories," the businessman says.
"The first bad story is about a mistake because of an animal noise."
"The second bad story is that I have pain in my body. The third bad story is now," the businessman says.
"Five hundred million of what?" the little prince asks again.
"Millions of those little bright things," he answers.
"Ah! You mean the stars?"
"Yes, that's it. The stars."

"And what do you do with five hundred million stars?"
"Nothing. I only own them."
"What good is it for you to own the stars?"
"It makes me rich."
"What good is it for you to be rich?"
"I can buy more stars."

"How can you own the stars?"

"There is no owner of the stars. When you find a diamond that belongs to nobody, it is yours. I own the stars because they have no owner."

"Yes, that is true, but what do you do with them?" the little prince asks.

"I count them and recount them."

"If I own an apple, I can eat it. But what can you do with the stars?" the little prince asks.

"I write the number of stars on a paper, and I can put the paper in the bank," the businessman answers.

"It sounds romantic but not important," the little prince thinks to himself. "I have a flower and three volcanoes. I take care of them, and that's what it means to own them. But you can't take care of the stars. Men are strange," the little prince says.

Chapter 14

The fifth star is the smallest. The star has a street lamp and a lamp-lighter.

"I think this man is less strange than the others," the little prince says to himself. "It is beautiful to turn the street lamp on and off. Beauty is truly useful."

"Good morning. Why do you turn off the lamp?" asks the little prince.

"That is the order," replies the lamplighter.

"What is the order?"

"The order is that I turn off my lamp."

"I don't understand," says the little prince.

"There is nothing to understand," says the lamplighter. "Orders are orders."

"I'm very sleepy. I don't have the rest of the night to sleep," the lamplighter says.

"Why not?" the little prince asks.

"Because this star moves faster and faster."

I follow a terrible profession.

"Then what?" asks the little prince.

"The star makes one turn every minute."

"What? A minute is a day here?" the little prince says with surprise.

"Yes, right now we are meeting for thirty minutes. Thirty minutes is a month, so we are meeting for a month!" the lamplighter says.

The little prince wants to help him. He is a true person.

"I can tell you a way you can rest whenever you want to..." The little prince continues,

"You can go all the way around this star in three steps. Just walk slowly, and it will still be daytime so that you can rest."

"That doesn't help. I want to sleep," says the lamplighter.

The little prince goes away. He thinks, "He's a wonderful person who works for others." The little prince says to himself, "I want to make friends with him, but his star is too small. There is no room for two people."

Chapter 15

The sixth star is very big. An old gentleman is writing a big book on the star.

"What is that big book? What are you doing?" asks the little prince.

"I am an earth scientist. An earth scientist knows the location of all the seas, rivers, and mountains," answers the old gentleman.

"That's a great job. Is there a sea on this star?"
"I don't know," the old man says.
"Ah! Then, what about a river or a mountain?"
"I don't know."
"But you are an earth scientist!"
"Yes, but I am not a traveler. An earth scientist cannot leave his desk."

The earth scientist says, "An earth scientist listens to a traveler and writes down what he hears in a book. The traveler's moral character is so important."
"Why is that?"
"If the traveler lies, this book becomes a fake book. A drunk person is not helpful to me."

"When I meet a traveler of good character, I ask for proof of what he finds.

But you...you come from far away! You are a traveler! Tell me about your star!" The scientist opens the book and he holds a pencil.

"My star is small," the little prince says. "My star has three volcanoes. I also have a flower."
"I do not write about flowers," the scientist says.
"Why is that?"
"This is a very important book. I can't change the story in this book. Flowers are short-lived. A mountain is more important than a live volcano or a dead volcano. A mountain does not change," the scientist says.

"But what does 'short-lived' mean?" the little prince asks.
"It means, it easily goes away." the scientist answers.
"My flower is 'short-lived,'" the little prince says to himself.
"Now she is alone on my star." He feels sorry.

"Go to the Earth," the scientist says.
So the little prince goes on his way, thinking of his flower.

Chapter 16

The seventh star is the Earth. Many people live here.

The Earth is large enough to need 462,511 lamplighters for the streets.

If you look at the lamplighters from a distance, they look like a ballet performance.

The lights turn on in New Zealand and Australia. Then, the lights turn on in China and Siberia. After that, the lights turn on in Russia, India, Africa, and Europe.

They don't make mistakes. It is amazing!

Chapter 17

The story of the lamplighters is not perfectly true. In fact, people can fill a very small place on Earth. But men don't believe me. They need time to think about numbers. However, you only have to believe me.

When the little prince comes to Earth, he sees something moving in the sand. It is a golden color.
"Good evening," says the little prince.
"Good evening," says the snake.
"What is this star?" asks the little prince.

When the little prince arrived on the Earth, he was very much surprised not to see any people.

"This is the Earth. This is Africa. This is the African desert, so there are no people here," the snake answers.

The little prince sits down on a stone and looks up to the sky. "Look at my star. It is right up there above us."
"It is beautiful, but what brings you here?" the snake asks.
"I have some trouble with a flower," answers the little prince.

"Where are the men? It is a little lonely in the desert..." the little prince says.
"It can also be lonely among men," the snake says.

The little prince looks at the snake for a long time. "I think you are not very powerful."
"No. I am very powerful. I can send anyone home at once," says the snake. "But you are weak, and you come from a star. I can help you someday if you are homesick, I can..."

Chapter 18

The little prince meets a flower in the desert.
"Good morning," says the little prince.
"Good morning," says the flower.

"Where are the men?" the little prince asks.
"I don't know where they are. Men don't have roots, so they move as the wind blows," the flower answers.

Chapter 19

It is altogether dry, and altogether pointed, and altogether harsh and forbidding.

After that, the little prince goes up a high mountain. He thinks, "If I go up to the top, I can see the people." But he sees only peaks of rocks.

"Good morning," he says simply.
"Good morning, Good morning, Good morning," answers the echo.
"What a strange star! It repeats what I say. My flower is the one that speaks to me first."

Chapter 20

Finally, the little prince comes to a town.

"Good morning," he says, standing before a garden.

"Good morning," say the roses.

"Who are you?"

"We are roses."

He remembers his flower telling him that she is the only one in the world, which makes him feel unhappy. "If my flower knows this, she can be very upset. Maybe she will say to me, 'I will die now.'"

"I think that I am rich, but I'm not. I have a common rose and three volcanoes. That doesn't make me a great prince." And he lies down in the grass and cries.

And he lay down in the grass and cried.

Chapter 21

Then, a fox comes to him, "Good morning." But the little prince sees nothing.

"I am under the apple tree," the voice says.

"Who are you?" asks the little prince.

"I am a fox," the fox says.

"Come and play with me. I am so unhappy," the little prince says.

"Sorry, I can't play with you. I am wild," the fox says.

"You don't live here. What are you looking for?"

"I'm looking for friends. What does 'wild' mean?" the little prince asks.

"It means 'not tame,'" the fox answers.

"What does 'tame' mean?"

"It means to be connected."

"To me, you are just one of many boys. And to you, I am just one of many foxes. But, if you tame me, I'm the only one to you in this world," the fox says.

"Ah! Now I understand. My flower on my star tames me," the little prince says.

"Another star? Are there chickens on that star?" the fox asks.

"No."

"Nothing is perfect."

"My life is very simple," the fox says.
"I hunt chickens. Men hunt me."

"But, if you tame me, your footsteps will sound like music to me," the fox says. "I don't eat bread, but if you tame me, I shall love those grain fields. They are golden like your hair color," the fox says.

The fox looks at the little prince, "Please! tame me!"
"I want to very much, but I can't," the little prince replies.
"I do not have much time. I need time to make friends."
"If you want a friend, tame me..." says the fox.

"What must I do to tame you?" asks the little prince.
"You must be very patient," the fox answers.
"First, you sit down a little away from me, then you sit a little closer to me every day."

The next day, the little prince comes back.
"It's good for me if you come back at the same time. I can

wait for that time," the fox says. "Also, we have to make a special day."

"A special day?" the little prince asks.

"Yes, we can make one day different from other days," the fox answers.

"For example, every Thursday, hunters play together in the village. Thursday is a special day for me! I can go everywhere freely."

"Ah, I understand," the little prince says.

At last, the little prince tames the fox. When they have to say goodbye, the fox feels sad.

"It is no good for you," the little prince says.

"No, it's not," says the fox. "Go and look again at the roses, then come back to say goodbye to me. I can tell you a secret."

The little prince goes to the roses. He says to the roses, "You're not at all like my rose. My rose is the only one in the world. You are beautiful, but you are empty," he goes on. "My rose is more important than all other roses, because I give her water. I put her under the glass cup. I listen to everything she says, because she is my rose."

He goes back to meet the fox. The fox says to him, "Here is my secret. The important things are what you can't see with your eyes." The fox goes on. "Time is important. Your rose is important to you, because you spend time with her."

Chapter 22

"Good morning. What do you do here?" says the little prince.

"I send off the trains to the right or the left," says the switchman.

A train is moving fast.

"What are they looking for?" the little prince asks.

The switchman says, "Nobody knows."

The second train is moving fast on the other side.

"Are they coming back already?"

"No, it is a different train."

The third train is moving fast.

"Are they following the first one?" asks the little prince.

"No, they are following nothing."

The little prince says, "Only the children know what they are looking for."

"Children are lucky," the switchman says.

Chapter 23

The little prince meets a seller. The seller sells a drug that makes you not need to drink any water.

"Why are you selling this?" the little prince asks.
"Because it saves time," the seller answers.

The little prince says to himself, "Hm...I want to use that time to find a spring of fresh water."

Chapter 24

On the eighth day, I listen to the story of the seller. I say to the little prince, "Your story is very interesting, but the plane is still not working and I have no more water to drink."

"My friend the fox..." the little prince says to me.
"This is not the time to talk about the fox. We are going to die."
He answers me, "It's good to have a friend, even if you're going to die."

He doesn't know how dangerous the situation is now, but he understands what I want, so we begin to walk.

It is night time already. Thirst makes me a little hot. "Are you thirsty too?" I ask.
He says, "Water may also be good for the heart..."

He sits down. He speaks again, "The stars are beautiful because there is a flower that no one can see."
The little prince goes on, "The desert is beautiful."
"Yes, that is true," I say.
"The desert is beautiful because there is water that you cannot see."

There is a treasure in my old house, but nobody can find that treasure. Yes, there are beautiful things you can't see with the eyes.

The little prince is asleep now. I walk on with the little prince. The moonlight shines on his face. It is like a treasure. The little prince touches my heart because of his unchanging heart for his flower. At last, the sun comes up. We find water.

He laughed, touched the rope, and set the pulley to working.

Chapter 25

"Men take the fast train, but they don't know what they're looking for," the little prince says.

We find a well, but this well is like a well in a town. It's like a dream.
"It is strange, everything is ready for us," I say to the little prince. The little prince touches the rope.

"Do you hear?" says the little prince, "The well wakes up, and it is singing..."
I say, "Give me this. It is too heavy for you."

I can see the sunlight on the water in the bucket.
"I am thirsty. Give me some water," the little prince says. He drinks the water. His eyes close. This water is good for the heart, like a gift.

"Men have many roses, but they can't find what they are looking for. You can find it in a rose or some water. You must look through your heart..." the little prince says.

I drink the water too. The color of sand is like honey.
"You must keep your promise," says the little prince.
"What promise?"
"A mask for my sheep."

I take my drawings out of my pocket. The little prince looks them over.

He laughs and says, "These baobab trees look like cabbages. The fox ears are too long."

"You are not nice," I say. "I am not good at drawing."

But, I draw a mask for his sheep.

"You have plans that I don't know about," I say.

He doesn't answer.

"My arrival was one year ago," says the little prince.

I don't know why, but I feel sad. "Are you traveling to that place?" I ask.

His face turns red. I go on, "Perhaps it is because of a special year?"

"Now you must return to your plane. Come back tomorrow evening..." the little prince says.

Chapter 26

Close to the well, there is an old stone wall. The little prince is sitting on top of the wall.

I hear his voice. "Yes, yes! It is the right day, but this is not the place."
I hear his voice again. "You have nothing to do. You wait for me there."
"You have good poison? Now go away," says the little prince. "I want to get down from the wall."

When I look at the foot of the wall, there is a yellow snake. That snake can take your life in just thirty seconds. I pull out a gun, but the snake goes away.

"Now, go away, I want to get down from the wall."

"Why are you talking with snakes?"

He doesn't answer.

I give him some water to drink. He puts his arms around my neck.

"I am glad that your plane is okay now," he says. "Now you can go back home. I am going back home today too. It is farther away. It is more difficult. I have your sheep. And I have the box. And I have the mask..."

I say to him, "You are afraid..."

He smiles lightly.

I say, "I want to hear you laugh again."

But he says to me, "Today marks a year. I can find my star."

He goes on, "The important things you cannot see."

I reply, "Yes, I know."

"If you see the star, there is a flower."

"Yes, I know."

"If you drink water, you can listen to music."

"Yes, I know."

"And at night you look up at the stars. You can't see my star, because it is so small, so you think that every star is my star."

He smiles again.

"Ah, little prince! I love to see that smile!"

"That is my gift, just that."

"Everyone has their stars. For travelers, the stars are guides.

For scientists, the stars are problems. But, for you, the star is laughing. I shall be laughing on my star because of you."

"You are always my friend. You can laugh with me anytime, but if your friends see you smiling at the sky, they think you are crazy. I give you a smile bell, not a star."

He quickly becomes serious.
"Tonight— you know — Do not come."
"I want to be with you tonight," I say.
He worries. "It is also because of the snake. He may bite you just for fun..."
"But I want to be with you tonight."

He goes away without a sound, but I catch up with him. He takes me by the hand. "It is wrong of you to come. You know, it is too far. I cannot carry this body with me.

And he sat down because he was afraid.

It is too heavy." He goes on. "But it's nice. I can hear the sound of water. You have a great many little bells and I have a great many wells."

"Here it is," the little prince says. He sits down. "You know, my flower... she is so weak. She needs me."
I sit down too.
"That is all..."
And he takes one step.
There is a yellow light close to his feet. He falls as gently as a tree falls.

Chapter 27

Six years pass by. I come home safely. My friends are happy about my safe return. I know he goes back to his star. At night, I love to listen to the little bells.

I forget to draw a rope to tie the mask. He can't put the mask on the sheep without a rope. Does the sheep eat the flower?

He fell as gently as a tree falls.

I say to myself, "No, the little prince puts a glass on the flower every evening, but what if he forgets one day? What if the sheep gets out at night, and eats the flower without a sound?"

It's interesting.
The world depends on whether the sheep eats the flower or not.

It is here that the little prince comes to Earth and goes away. Look at it carefully. Maybe the little prince will come back. If you meet the little prince, please let me know.

Level 2는 Level 1 문장에서 동사 시제를 원문과 동일하게 바꿨어요.
동사 시제 변형이 어려운 분들은 Level 1과 비교하며 읽어보세요.
변형되는 동사의 모습을 쉽게 찾을 수 있습니다.
Level 1에서 현재 동사로 표현할 수 없는 문장들이 추가됐어요.

In Level 2, the verb tenses of the Level 1 book are changed to the same verbs used in the original copy. For those who are having a hard time with the changed verb tenses, try comparing them with the Level 1 book. You could find the verbs easily this way. Sentences that cannot be expressed with present tenses are added in the Level 2 book.

THE ORIGINAL TEXT

Once when I was six years old, I saw a magnificent picture in a book, called True Stories from Nature, about the primeval forest. It was a picture of a boa constrictor in the act of swallowing an animal. Here is a copy of the drawing.

·
·
·
·
·

LEVEL 2

I saw a big snake in a book.
The snake ate an animal.

Chapter 1

I saw a big snake in a book. The snake ate an animal.

After eating an animal, this snake does not need to eat for six months.

I drew that big snake. This is drawing number one.

But the man said, "This is a drawing of a hat."

My drawing was not of a hat, so I drew a picture of an elephant inside a snake. This is drawing number two.

The man said to me, "Stop drawing. Just do other things." So, I gave up being a painter.

Now I am a pilot. I have flown to many cities around the world.

I met many great people, but my mind did not change.

When I met a smart person, I showed him drawing number one.

The person said, "That is a hat."

After that, I would never talk to that person about big snakes or the jungle. I would talk about card games and golf to make him happy.

Chapter 2

I had no friends to talk to until six years ago.

At that time, my plane stopped working in the desert. There was only me. Also, I had only water for one week.

On the first night, I slept on the sand. I heard a strange little voice in the morning.
"Draw me a sheep."
"What?"

There was a child who looked at me carefully. Here is a drawing of him. He looks sweeter than in my drawing because I stopped drawing when I was six years old.

I looked at the child with surprise. This was the desert. The child didn't seem lost in the desert.

I said, "What are you doing here?"
He repeated, "Draw me a sheep."

So I took out a sheet of paper and a pen, but I was still in the desert.

As you know, I did not know how to draw, but he said to me,
"That doesn't matter. Draw me a sheep..."

I didn't draw a sheep, but I drew the boa snake.

Then he said, "No, no! I do not want an elephant inside a boa snake. I need a sheep. Draw me a sheep."

So I drew a sheep.
But he said to me, "No, this sheep is already very sickly."

So, I drew another one once more.
But he rejected that too.

I drew another one in a hurry.
"This is the box. The sheep is inside it."

He said with a bright smile, "That is exactly what I want. Does this sheep eat a lot?"
"Why?"
"Because in my place, everything is very small."

I said, "He is a very small sheep. There is enough grass for him."
He said, "He's not that small... Look! He's fallen asleep."

Chapter 3

I got to know the little prince little by little.

When he saw my airplane, he asked, "What is that?"
"That is an airplane. It can fly."

He cried out, "What! You dropped down from the sky?"
I answered softly, "Yes."
"Oh! That's funny! Ha Ha!"

"So you come from the sky too! Where is your star?"
I was surprised, so I asked him quickly. "Do you come from another star?" But he did not answer.

He looked at the plane and said, "You can't have come from very far away..."
After a time, he carefully took the drawing of the sheep out of his pocket.
Other stars? I asked many questions.

"Where do you come from? Where do you want to take your sheep?"
He said, "This box is the sheep's house at night."

"If you are good, I will give you a rope to tie the sheep."
"Tie the sheep? That is strange."
"But if you don't tie the sheep, he will go away."
"It is okay because my star is so small."

Chapter 4

Now I had more information about the little prince. His star was about the size of a house.

When a star scientist finds a small star, he gives it a name by giving it a number. I believe the little prince came from star B-612.

A Turkish star scientist found this star, but nobody believed his words because he was wearing Turkish clothes.

A Turkish leader had great power. He ordered his people to change from Turkish clothes to European clothes. The star scientist was wearing European clothes and talked about B-612 again. After this, everybody believed his words.

I talked about numbers a lot because men like numbers. When you tell them that you have made a new friend, they ask you these questions: "How old is he?" "How many brothers does he have?"

They always want to know about numbers.

If you talked to men, you would have to tell them, "I saw a house that cost $20,000."
Then they would say, "Oh, what a pretty house that is!"

If you said to them, "There was the little prince; he was lovely, and he was looking for a sheep."
They would consider you to be a child.

But if you said to them, "The star he came from is B-612," they could understand what you said.

I would have liked to begin this story like a fairy tale, but then people would read it lightly and forget about it.

My friend went away six years ago. I don't want to forget the little prince, so I'm describing him here. This is why I bought a box of paints and pencils, but it's not easy for me to draw again at my age.

Sometimes I make some errors, but I try to draw as well as I can. I may make mistakes on important details, but that will not be my fault, because my friend never explained anything to me. Maybe I am a little more like men now.

Chapter 5

On the third day, I heard a story about the problem of the baobabs. (This is a tree name.)

The little prince asked me quickly, "Is it true that sheep eat little trees?"
"Yes, that is true."
"Ah! I am glad!"

"Do they also eat baobab trees?" The little prince asked me again.
I said to him, "No, baobabs are not little trees. They are as big as castles."
But he said wisely, "Before they are so big, the baobabs start by being little."
"Yes, that's right."
"But why do you want the sheep to eat the little baobabs?"
"What are you talking about?"

He did not answer, so I had to find an answer by myself. Maybe there was also good grass and bad grass on his star. If he saw bad grass, he had to pull them out fast. There were very bad seeds on the star. They were baobab seeds. If baobabs are pulled out late, they split the star into pieces.

The little prince said to me later, "You have to pull out baobabs, just like how you wash your face every day.
It's boring, but it's easy."

The baobabs.

One day he said to me, "Draw a picture and let the children know about this land. If you don't do it every day, you will have big problems."

So I drew a star that was being broken by baobab trees. "Children! Watch out for the baobabs!" I drew that tree very carefully. I think this drawing is excellent.

I tried to draw other pictures along with the baobabs, but I couldn't. The other pictures were not as good as the picture of the baobabs.

Chapter 6

Oh, little prince! Little by little, I came to understand your sad and little life.

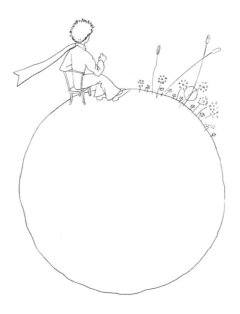

On the fourth day, I got to know the little prince more. The little prince's star is so small, he can see the sunset at any time.

If he wants to see the sunset, he only needs to move his chair a few steps forward.

"One day," he said to me, "I saw the sunset 44 times!"

Chapter 7

On the fifth day, he suddenly asked me, "Does a sheep eat flowers too?"

I answered him, "A sheep eats anything."

"A sheep eats roses?"

"Yes, sure."

"But roses have thorns that are guarding it."

I was very much worried about fixing the plane, so I couldn't answer.

"Then, what use are thorns?"

I answered with the first thing that came into my head.

"The thorns are no use at all."

"I don't believe you! Roses are weak, so they have thorns. They think that thorns are perfect weapons, and you really believe that the flowers..."

I cried out, "No, no! I don't believe anything. Don't you see? I am very busy. I am fixing the plane. This is very important work for me."

He looked at me, "Important work? You talk just like the men! You mix everything up together..." He was very angry.

"I know a man. He has never loved anyone. He only loves numbers. All day he says over and over, just like you, 'I am busy. I do important work.'"

"It is difficult for flowers to make thorns. But do you think that is not important? Is the war between the sheep and the flowers not important?"

"There is only one flower in the world, but one little sheep can destroy it in a bite. You think that is not important!"

"If someone loves a flower, that flower is the only one in the world. He is happy just thinking about that flower. But, if the sheep eats that flower, he loses everything. You think that is not important!"

He cried with no sounds. I dropped my tools. I took him in my arms. I said to him, "The flower that you love is not in danger. I can draw a mask for your sheep. I can..." I didn't know what to say to him.

Chapter 8

On the little prince's star, the flowers were very simple. The flowers came out from the grass and went away peacefully.

One day something came out of the ground. It had small leaves. The little prince watched those small leaves very closely.

The plant got ready to make a flower. The flower prepared to show her beauty in her flower room. She chose her flower colors carefully. She wanted to come out when it was full of beautiful light. She was a very lovely plant.

The flower took a long time to prepare. Finally, she came out. But the flower said, "I just woke up. I don't look good." The little prince said to her, "Oh! How beautiful you are!" "Sure, I am. I was born at the same time as the sun." "I think it's time to eat," the flower said. "Please think about my needs." The little prince brought her fresh water.

One day the flower said, "I'm not afraid of tigers. I have four thorns."

"Tigers don't eat plants." said the little prince. "Well..." She changed her words. "I don't like the wind. I want you to place me under a glass cup. It is very cold here." She coughed two times. "The glass cup?"

The little prince loved the flower with all his heart, but he was unhappy because he thought deeply about what she said.

The little prince shared his thoughts with me. "I should not have listened to what she said. I should have smelled the flower. That's enough. However, the truth is that I didn't know how to understand anything. I should never have run away from her... But I was too young to know how to love her..."

Chapter 9

The little prince cleaned two active volcanoes before leaving his star. He cleaned the third volcano. The third volcano didn't work anymore. If you clean them well, volcanoes will be okay.

He removed the little baobabs. He watered the flower. He felt that he was very close to tears.

"Goodbye," he said to the flower.
She didn't answer.
At last she said to him, "Could you forgive me? And be happy... I love you too. Try to be happy... I don't need the glass cup anymore."

"But the wind..."
"The cool night air will do me good. I am a flower."
"But the animals..."
"It's okay. Don't worry about that. Just go." She didn't want him to see her crying.

Chapter 10

The little prince visited stars 325-330.

On the first star, there was a king. When the king saw the little prince, he said, "Ah! Here is a citizen."

Every man is a citizen of the king, so the king called, "Ah! Here is a citizen." The king said, "Come closer to me."

The little prince wanted to sit down, but he kept standing because there was no place to sit.

The little prince yawned, but the king stopped him.
"I'm sleepy, so I can't stop myself."
"Ah, then, I command you to yawn," the king said.
"Your command scares me... I can't."
"Then, I... I command..." The king became a little angry because he had great power and everyone must accept his commands.

He was a good king because he made his commands reasonable.
"May I sit down?" the little prince asked.
"I command you to do so," the king answered.

The little prince thought, "This star is so small."
"Lord," he said to the king. "Over what do you rule?"

"Over everything," said the king.

"Over everything?" asked the little prince.

"Yes, Over everything on every star," the king answered.

"The stars obey you?"

"Certainly, they do," the king said.

The little prince thought, "What a great power." If he had such power, he wouldn't need to move his chair to watch the sunset. He felt a bit sad. He remembered his star.

"I want to see the sunset," the little prince said.

"If I ordered a general to carry out an impossible command, who would be wrong? the general or I?"

"You," said the little prince.

"That's right," the king said. "The command should be acceptable."

"What about my sunset?" the little prince asked.

"You shall have your sunset, but you shall have to wait," the king answered.

"Until when?"

"Hmm, let me see. This evening, around twenty minutes to eight."

"I have nothing more to do here," he said to the king. "I will go on my way again."

"Do not go," said the king. "I will make you Minister of Law!"

"But there is nobody here to judge!" the little prince said.

"Then you shall judge yourself," the king said to the little prince.

"But I can judge myself anywhere."

"Well then, you can judge the old mouse on our star. It's okay to give him the death penalty."

"I don't want to put anyone to death. I need to go on my way."

"No," said the king.

"If you command me to go, I will follow your command," the little prince said.

But the king had no answer. So the little prince went on his way.

Chapter 11

A big talker lived on the second star. When he saw the little prince, he said, "Ah! Ah! You have come to respect me."

"You wear a strange hat," said the little prince.
"This hat is for welcoming visitors," he replied.

"Clap your hands," he said to the little prince. The little prince clapped his hands. Then he took off his hat. The little prince and the big talker repeated these actions for five minutes.
"What should I do to make the hat fall to the ground?" the little prince asked.

He could only listen to good words. "Do you really respect me?" said the big talker.
"What does that mean, 'respect'?" the little prince asked.
"To respect means to believe 'you are the best in every way.'"

"But you are the only man on your star! Even if I respect you, what is the point? You are the only one." The little prince went away.

Chapter 12

There was a drunk person on the third star.
"What are you doing there?" the little prince asked.

"I am drinking," he replied.
"Why are you drinking?"
"I want to forget."
"Forget what?" the little prince asked again.
"Forget that I feel bad," he said.
"Feel bad for what?"
"Feel bad for drinking!" he answered.

"Men are very, very strange," the little prince thought as he went away.

Chapter 13

There was a businessman on the fourth star. "Good morning," the little prince said to him. But he didn't answer.

"Three and two make five. Good morning. Fifteen and seven make twenty-two. Phew! Then that totals five-hundred-and-one million..."

"Five hundred million of what?" asked the little prince.
"Eh? Are you still there? I do very important work."
"Five hundred million of what?" asked the little prince again.

"I've made three mistakes so far," the businessman said.
"The first thing was that I made a mistake because of an animal noise."
"And the second bad story was that I had pain in my body. The third one is now," the businessman said.
"Five hundred million of what?" the little prince asked again.
"Millions of those little bright things," he answered.
"Ah! You mean the stars?"
"Yes, that's it. The stars."

"What do you do with five-hundred million stars?"
"Nothing. I only own them."
"What good is it for you to own the stars?"
"It makes me rich."
"What good is it for you to be rich?"

"I can buy more stars."

"How is it possible to own the stars?"

"There is no owner of the stars. When you find a diamond that belongs to nobody, it is yours. I owned the stars because they have no owner."

"Yes, that is true, but what do you do with them?" said the little prince.

"I count them and recount them."

"If I own an apple, I can eat it, but what can you do with the stars?" asked the little prince.

"I write the number of stars on a paper and I put that paper in the bank," the businessman answered.

"It sounds romantic but not important," thought the little prince. "I have a flower and three volcanoes. I take care of them and that's what it means to own them. But you can't take care of the stars. Men are strange," the little prince said.

Chapter 14

The fifth star was the smallest. The star had a street lamp and a lamp-lighter.

"I think this man is less strange than the others," the little prince said to himself.

"It is beautiful to turn the street lamp on and off. Beauty is truly useful."

"Good morning. Why do you turn off the lamp?" said the little prince.

"That is the order," replied the lamplighter.

"What is the order?"

"The order is that I turn off my lamp."

"I do not understand," said the little prince.

"There is nothing to understand," said the lamplighter.

"Orders are orders."

"I'm very sleepy. I don't have the rest of the night to sleep," the lamplighter said.

"Why not?" the little prince asked.

"Because this star moves faster and faster."

"Then what?" asked the little prince.

"The star makes one turn every minute."

"What? One minute is a day?" the little prince was surprised.

"Yes, now we have met for thirty minutes. Thirty minutes is a month, so we have met for a month!" the lamplighter said.

Because he was a true person, the little prince wanted to help him.
"I can tell you a way you can rest whenever you want to..." The little prince continued,

I follow a terrible profession.

"You can go all the way around this star in three steps. Just walk slowly, and it will be daytime so that you can rest."
"That doesn't help. I want to sleep," said the lamplighter.

The little prince went away. He thought that, "he's a wonderful person who works for others." The little prince said to himself,
"I want to make friends with him, but his star is too small. There is no room for two people."

Chapter 15

The sixth star was very large, and an old gentleman was writing a big book on the star.

"What is that big book? And what are you doing?" asked the little prince.

"I am an earth scientist. An earth scientist knows the location of all the seas, rivers, and mountains," answered the old gentleman.

"That's a great job. Is there a sea on this star?"
"I don't know," the old man said.
"Ah! Then, what about a river or a mountain?"
"I don't know."
"But you are an earth scientist!"
"Yes, but I am not a traveler. An earth scientist cannot leave his desk."

The earth scientist said, "An earth scientist listens to a traveler and writes it down in a book. That's why the traveler's moral character is so important."
"Why is that?"
"If the traveler lies, this book becomes a fake book. A drunk person is not helpful to me."

"When I met a traveler of good character, I asked for proof of what he found. But you...you come from far away!

You are a traveler! Tell me about your star!" The scientist opened the book and he held a pencil.

"My star is small," the little prince said. "My star has three volcanoes. I also have a flower."
"I do not write about flowers," the scientist said.
"Why is that?"

"This is a very important book. I can't change the story in this book. Flowers have a short life span. A mountain is more important than a live volcano or a dead volcano. A mountain does not change," the scientist said.

"But what does that mean 'short life span?'" the little prince asked.
"It means it easily dies," the scientist answered.
"My flower has a 'short life span,'" the little prince said to himself. "Now she is alone on my star." He felt sorry.

"Go to the Earth," the scientist said.
So the little prince went on his way, thinking of his flower.

Chapter 16

The seventh star was the Earth. A lot of people are living here.

The Earth is large enough to need 462,511 lamplighters for the streets.

If you look at the lamplighters from a distance, they look like a ballet performance.

The lights turn on in New Zealand and Australia. Then, the lights turn on in China and Siberia. After that, the lights turn on in Russia, India, Africa and Europe.

They don't make mistakes. It is amazing!

Chapter 17

The story of the lamplighters was not perfectly true. In fact, people could fill a very small place on Earth. But men don't believe me. They need time to think about numbers. However, you only have to believe me.

When the little prince came to Earth, he saw something moving in the sand. It was a golden color.
"Good evening," said the little prince.

"You are a funny animal,
you are no thicker than a finger..."

"Good evening," said the snake.

"What is this star?" asked the little prince.

"This is the Earth. This is Africa. This is the African desert, so there are no people here," the snake answered.

The little prince sat down on a stone and looked up to the sky. "Look at my star. It is right there above us."

"It is beautiful, but what brings you here?" the snake asked.

"I had some trouble with a flower," answered the little prince.

"Where are the men? It is a little lonely in the desert..." the little prince said.

"It is also lonely among men," the snake said.

The little prince looked at the snake for a long time. "I think you are not very powerful."

"No. I'm very powerful. I can send anyone home at once," said the snake. "But you are weak, and you come from a star. I can help you someday if you are homesick, I can..."

Chapter 18

The little prince met a flower in the desert.
"Good morning," said the little prince.
"Good morning," said the flower.

"Where are the men?" the little prince asked.
"I don't know where to meet them. Men don't have roots, so they go away as the wind blows," the flower answered.

Chapter 19

After that, the little prince went up a high mountain. He thought, "If I go up to the top, I can see the people." But he saw nothing, only peaks of rocks.

"Good morning," he simply said.
"Good morning, Good morning, Good morning," answered the echo.
"What a strange star! It repeats what I say. My flower spoke to me first."

Chapter 20

Finally, the little prince came to a town.
"Good morning," he said, standing before a garden.
"Good morning," said the roses.

"Who are you?"
"We are roses."
His flower told him that she was the only one in the world,
so he felt unhappy. "If my flower knew this, she would be
very upset. Maybe she would say to me, 'I am going to die
now.'"

The little prince thought, "I was rich. But I'm not. I had a
common rose and three volcanoes; that doesn't make
me a great prince." He lay down in the grass and cried.

Chapter 21

Then a fox came to him, "Good morning." The little prince could not see anything.

"I am under the apple tree," the voice said.

"Who are you?" asked the little prince.

"I am a fox," the fox said.

"Come and play with me. I am so unhappy," the little prince said.

"Sorry, I can't play with you. I am wild," the fox said.

"You do not live here. What are you looking for?"

"I am looking for friends. What does 'wild' mean?" the little prince asked.

"It means 'not tame,'" the fox replied.

"What does 'tame' mean?"

"It means to be connected."

"You are just one of many boys to me. And I am also just one of many foxes to you. But, if you tame me, I'm the only one to you in this world," the fox said.

"Ah! I understand now. My flower on my star tamed me," the little prince said.

"Another star? Are there chickens on that star?" the fox asked.

"No."

"Nothing is perfect."

"My life is very simple," the fox said.
"I hunt chickens. Men hunt me."

"But, if you tame me,
your footsteps will
sound like music
to me," the fox
said. "I do not
eat bread, but
if you tame me,
I shall love those
grain fields. Those
grain fields are golden like your hair color," the fox said.

The fox looked at the little prince, "Please! tame me!"
"I very much want to, but I can't," the little prince replied.
"I do not have much time. I need time to make friends."
"If you want a friend, tame me..." said the fox.

"What must I do to tame you?" asked the little prince.
"You must be very patient," the fox answered.
"First, you will sit down a little distance away from me, then
you will sit a little closer to me every day."

The next day, the little prince came back.
"It would be better to come back at the same hour. I shall
feel happier and happier as that time comes," the fox
said. "Also, we have to make a special day."

"A special day?" the little prince asked.

"Yes, we can make one day different from other days," the fox answered.

"For example, every Thursday, the hunters play together in the village. Thursday is a special day for me! I can go everywhere freely."

"Ah, I understand," the little prince said.

At last, the little prince tamed the fox. When they had to say goodbye, the fox felt sad.

"It's no good for you," the little prince said.

"No, it's not," said the fox. "Go and look again at the roses, then come back to say goodbye to me. I can tell you a secret."

The little prince went to the roses. He said to the roses, "You're not at all like my rose. My rose is the only one in the world. You are beautiful, but you are empty," he went on. "My rose is more important than all other roses, because I have watered her. I put her under the glass cup. I listened to everything she said, because she is my rose."

He went back to meet the fox. The fox said to him, "Here is my secret. The important things are what can't be seen with your eyes." The fox went on. "Time is important. Your rose is important to you because you spend time with her."

Chapter 22

"Good morning. What are you doing here?" said the little prince.

"I send off the trains to the right or the left," said the switchman.

A train was moving fast.

"What are they looking for?" the little prince asked.

The switchman said, "Nobody knows."

The second train was moving fast on the other side.

"Are they coming back already?"

"No, it is a different train."

The third train was moving fast.

"Are they following the first one?" asked the little prince.

"No, they are following nothing."

The little prince said, "Only the children know what they are looking for."

"Children are lucky," the switchman said.

Chapter 23

The little prince met a seller. The seller sold a drug that makes you not need to drink any water.

"Why are you selling this?" the little prince asked.
"Because it saves time," the seller answered.

The little prince said to himself, "Hm...I want to use that time to find a spring of fresh water."

Chapter 24

On the eighth day, I listened to the story of the seller. I said to the little prince, "Your story is very interesting, but the plane is still not working and I have no more water to drink."

"My friend the fox..." the little prince said to me.
"This is not the time to talk about the fox. We are going to die."
He answered me,
"It's good to have a friend, even if you're going to die."

He didn't know how dangerous the situation was, but he understood what I wanted, so we started walking.

It was night time already. Thirst had made me a little hot.
"Are you thirsty too?" I asked.
He said, "Water may also be good for the heart..."

He sat down. He spoke again, "The stars are beautiful because there is a flower that cannot be seen."
The little prince went on, "The desert is beautiful."
"Yes, that's true," I said.
"The desert is beautiful because there is water that you cannot see."

There was a treasure in my old house, but nobody could find that treasure. Yes, beautiful things can't be seen with the eyes.

The little prince fell asleep. I carried on, with the little prince by my side. The moonlight shone on his face. It was like a treasure. The little prince touched my heart. It was because of his unchanging heart for his flower. At last, the sun came up. We found water.

He laughed, touched the rope, and set the pulley to working.

Chapter 25

"Men take the fast train, but they don't know what they're looking for," the little prince said.

We found a well, but this well was like a well in a town. It was like a dream.

"It is strange, everything is ready for us," I said to the little prince. The little prince touched the rope.

"Do you hear?" said the little prince, "The well has woken up and is singing..."

I said, "Let me take this. It's too heavy for you."

I could see the sunlight on the water in the bucket.

"I am thirsty. Give me some water," the little prince said. He drank the water. He closed his eyes. This water was good for the heart, like a gift. When I was a little boy, I received gifts. The lights on the Christmas tree had made the gift I received more beautiful.

"Men have many roses, but they can't find what they are looking for. It could be in a rose or some water. You must look with the heart..." the little prince said.

I drank the water too. The color of the sand was like honey.

"You must keep your promise," said the little prince.

"What promise?"

"A mask for my sheep."

I took my drawings out of my pocket. The little prince looked them over.

He laughed and said, "These baobab trees look like cabbages. The fox ears are too long."

"You are not nice," I said. "I'm not good at drawing."

But I drew a mask for his sheep.

"You have plans I don't know about," I said.

He didn't answer.

"I came down here a year ago," the little prince said.

I didn't know why, but I felt sad. "Were you on your way to the place where you landed?" I asked.

His face turned red. I went on, "Perhaps it was because of a special year?"

His face turned red once more.

"Now you must return to your plane. Come back tomorrow evening..." the little prince said.

Chapter 26

Close to the well, there was an old stone wall. The little prince was sitting on top of the wall.

I heard his voice say, "Yes, yes! It is the right day, but this is not the place."
I heard his voice again. "You have nothing else to do. Wait for me there."
"You have good poison? Now go away," said the little prince. "I want to come down from the wall."

When I looked at the foot of the wall, there was a yellow snake. That snake could end your life in just thirty seconds. I pulled out a gun, but the snake went away.

"Why are you talking with snakes?"
He didn't answer.
I gave him some water to drink. He put his arms around my neck.

"I am glad that your plane is okay now," he said. "Now you can go back home. I am going back home today too. It is much farther away. It is more difficult. I have your sheep, the box, snd the mask..."
I said to him, "You are afraid..."
He smiled lightly.

I said, "I want to hear you laugh again."

But he said to me,

"Today is one year. I can find my star." He went on, "The important things are things that cannot be seen."

I replied, "Yes, I know."

"If you see the star, there is a flower."

"Yes, I know."

"If you drink water, you can listen to music."

"Yes, I know."

"And at night you look up at the stars. You can't see my star, because it is so small, so you think that every star is my star."

He smiled again.

"Ah, little prince! I love to see that smile!"

"That is my gift, just that."

"Everyone has their own stars. For travelers, stars are guides. For scientists, they are problems. But for you, the star will be laughing. I shall be laughing on my star because of you."

"You will always be my friend. You will want to laugh with me, but if your friends see you smiling at the sky, they will think you are crazy. I gave you a smile bell, not a star."

He quickly became serious.

"Tonight - you know - Do not come."

"I want to be with you tonight," I said.

He was worried. "It is also because of the snake. He may bite you just for fun..."

"But I shall not leave you."

He went away without a sound, but I caught up with him. He took me by the hand. "It was wrong of you to come. You know, it's too far. I cannot carry this body with me. It is too heavy." He went on, "But it's nice. I can hear the sound of water. You have a great many little bells and I have a great many wells."

"Here it is," the little prince said. He sat down. "You know my flower... she is so weak. She needs me."

I sat down too.

"That is all..."

He took one step. There was a yellow light close to his feet. He fell as gently as a tree falls.

Chapter 27

Six years have already passed by. I went back home safely. My friends were happy about my safe return. I know he went back to his star. At night, I love to listen to the little bells.

I forgot to draw a rope to tie the mask. He might not have been able to put a mask on the sheep. Did the sheep eat the flower?

I said to myself, "No, the little prince covered the flower with the glass cup every evening, but what if he forgot one day? What if the sheep got out without a sound during the night?"

It's interesting.
The world depends on whether the sheep ate the flowers or not. Did the sheep eat it? Did the sheep not eat it?

This is where the little prince came to Earth and went away. Look at it carefully. Maybe the little prince will come back. If you ever meet the little prince, please let me know.

Level 3은 여전히 쉬운 단어를 사용하지만
원문을 이해하는데 필요한 핵심 정보들이 추가 되었어요.
Level 2를 읽고 여기까지 오셨다면 어렵지 않게 읽을 수 있습니다.

Level 3 book still uses easy words.
However, key information is added to understand the original story.
If you have read the Level 2 book, then it will not be difficult for you to
read the Level 3 book.

THE ORIGINAL TEXT

The fifth planet was very strange. It was the smallest of all. There was just enough room on it for a street lamp and a lamplighter. The little prince was not able to reach any explanation of the use of a street lamp and a lamplighter, somewhere in the heavens, on a planet which had no people, and not one house.

LEVEL 3

The fifth planet was very strange. It was the small-est of all. There was just enough space for a street lamp and a lamplighter. The little prince could not understand why a street lamp was needed on such a small planet.

The Little Prince
LEVEL 3 🔖🔖🔖

어린왕자 레벨3

Chapter 1

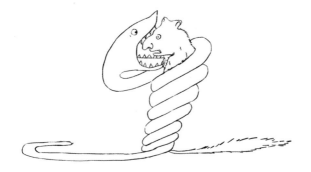

When I was six years old, I saw an excellent picture in a book. It was a picture of a snake eating an animal. The book said,

"These snakes do not bite when they eat animals. After eating, this snake does not need to eat for six months."

I loved that book, so I read it carefully. I drew a picture with a pencil. This was my first drawing. I called it "The Big Snake That Ate A Big Elephant."

I showed my drawing to the grown-ups.

I asked them, "Is this scary?"

They said, "This is a hat. The hat is not scary."

My drawing was not of a hat. My drawing was a drawing of a big snake after eating an elephant, but they didn't understand. I drew another picture to show the elephant inside the snake. This was my drawing number two. They could understand drawing number two.

But they said to me, "Stop painting. Just do other things. History or geography is good for you."

I felt unhappy about drawing number one and two, so I gave up being a painter at the age of six. It is hard for children to explain everything to the grown-ups.

Finally, I became a pilot. I have flown to many cities around the world. And it is true that geography is very useful to me. I now know where China and Arizona are on the map. I have met many great people. I got to know those people closely, but my opinion didn't change.

I kept my drawing number one. When I would meet a smart person, I would show them drawing number one. He or she would always say, "That is a hat."

Then I would never talk to that person about big snakes, jungles, or stars. I would bring myself down to his level. I would talk about card games, golf, politics, or neckties to make him happy.

Chapter 2

I lived my life alone until I had an accident in the desert six years ago.

Something broke in my engine. I was alone, without any engineers or passengers. It was a question of life or death for me. I had only enough water for a week.

On the first night, I went to sleep on the sand, a thousand miles from a town. I was alone, like a man who is on the ocean in a broken ship. At sunrise, a strange little voice woke me up.

"Draw me a sheep!"
"What?"
"Draw me a sheep!"

I jumped to my feet. I blinked my eyes hard. I looked carefully all around me. I saw a small person, who looked at me with great seriousness. Here you can see the best drawing I could make of him.

My drawing is less lovely than its model. However, that is not my fault. The grown-ups crushed my dream of being a painter when I was six years old, and I never learned how to draw anything.

Now I looked at this unexpected situation, wide-eyed in surprise.
Remember? I had just crashed in the desert.

Nevertheless, my little man did not seem to be lost in the desert. He didn't seem afraid of tiredness, hunger, thirst, or fear. Nothing about him hinted that he was a lost child in the desert.

I said to him: "What are you doing here?"
He repeated, very slowly, as if he was speaking of something important, "If you please... draw me a sheep..."

A strange mood overpowered me. As crazy as it seemed, I was still in the desert, a thousand miles from any town. I took a sheet of paper and a pen out of my pocket.

I remembered studying geography, history, and grammar, so I told the little man, "I don't know how to draw."
He answered me, "That doesn't matter. Draw me a sheep..."

But since I had never drawn a sheep, I drew the boa snake for him instead. It was a drawing of a boa snake from the outside, and I was surprised to hear,
"No, no! I do not want an elephant inside a boa snake. Where I live, everything is very small. What I need is a sheep. Draw me a sheep."

So I made another drawing, but he said, "No, this sheep looks very sickly. Make me another one." So I made another drawing. Then he said, "This is not a sheep. This is a male sheep." So I did my drawing over once more, but it was rejected too, just like the others.

By this time, my patience had run out because I was in a hurry to fix my engine. I drew quickly. I explained to him, "This is a box. The sheep is inside."

I was surprised to see his face become bright, "That is exactly what I wanted! Do you think that this sheep will eat lots of grass?"

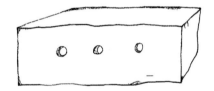

"Why?"
"Because where I live, everything is very small..."

"There will be enough grass for him," I said. "He is a very small sheep." He looked at the drawing. "Not so small, though... Look! He's fallen asleep..."

Chapter 3

It took a long time to learn where the little prince came from. He asked me so many questions, but he didn't seem to hear my questions. Little by little, I got to know everything from the words he told me by chance.

For example, the first time he saw my airplane, he asked me, "What is that thing?"
"That is not a thing. It flies. It is an airplane. It is my airplane." It felt good to tell him that I could fly.

He cried out, "What! You dropped down from the sky?"
"Yes," I answered gently. "Oh! That is funny!" Suddenly the little prince began to laugh in a lovely way. The laughter made me unhappy. I wanted to be taken seriously.

Then he added, "So you come from the sky too! Where is your planet?" At that moment, I caught a hint from his story. "Do you come from another planet?" But he did not reply.

He looked up gently while looking at my plane. "It is true that you could not have come from very far away..."

He thought deeply for a long time. Then, taking the drawing of the sheep out of his pocket, he looked carefully at his precious drawing. You can understand my interest in him. When he talked to me about "other planets," I tried to learn about this subject.

"My little man, where do you come from? What do you mean, 'where I live'? Where do you want to take your sheep?"
After a time, he answered, "The box you have given me can be used for his house at night."

"That's right. If you are good, I will give you a string too. You can tie him during the day on a fence."
The little prince was shocked, "Tie him? What a strange idea!"

"If you don't tie him," I said, "he will go somewhere and get lost."
My friend broke into another laugh, "But where do you think he would go?"
"Anywhere."
Then the little prince said, "That doesn't matter. My planet is so small!"

Chapter 4

I had learned a second fact. That the little prince's planet was a little bit larger than a house! That did not really surprise me much. There are also hundreds of small planets. Those planets are hard to see using a telescope.

When a space scientist discovers a small planet, he does not give it a name, he gives it only a number. I believe that the little prince came from a small planet named B-612.

This planet discovered by a Turkish space scientist using a telescope. The space scientist presented it to other scientists, but he was wearing Turkish clothes, so nobody believed what he said.

A Turkish ruler made a law. His law was that everyone must wear European clothes. So in 1920, the space scientist gave his presentation again. Dressed in European clothes, his report was finally accepted.

If I have told you these details about the small planet, it is because of the men and their ways. When you tell them that you have made a new friend, they never ask you, "What does his voice sound like? What games does he love best?" Instead, they ask you, "How old is he? How many brothers does he have? How much does he weigh?" They think they have learned everything about him from numbers.

If you said to the grown-ups,
"I saw a beautiful house made of red brick with flowerpots
in the windows," they could not get any idea of that house.
You would have to say to them,
"I saw a house that cost $20,000." Then they would shout,
"Oh, what a pretty house that is!"

If you say to them, "The fact that the little prince existed is
that he was lovely, and he was looking for a sheep," they
would treat you like a child.

However, if you said to them, "The planet he came from is
B-612," then they would believe it. They are like that, but
you shouldn't blame them. Children should always have
great patience with them.

I would have liked to begin this story as a fairy tale. I
would have liked to say, "Once upon a time, there was
a little prince who lived
on a planet and wanted
a sheep..." To those who
understand life, that would
have given more truth
to my story. I don't want
anyone to read my book
lightly.

Six years have already passed since my friend went away with his sheep. I try to make sure that I do not forget him. To forget a friend is sad. If I forget him, I may become like the grown-ups who love numbers...

This is why I have bought a box of paints and some pencils. It's hard to start drawing again at my age. I have not made any pictures except the boa snake since I was six.

I will certainly try to make the pictures as true as possible, but I am not at all sure of my success. I made some errors in the little prince's height. In one place he is too tall and in another, too short. So, I draw him step by step as best I can. I hope it will look normal.

I may make mistakes on important details, but that is not my fault. My friend never explained anything to me. He thought that I was like him, but I'm not. I can't see sheep through the box. Maybe I am a little more like the grown-ups.

Chapter 5

As each day passed, I would learn something about the little prince's planet. The information would come very slowly. On the third day, I learned about the problem of the baobabs. Once again, I thanked the sheep.

The little prince asked me quickly, "Is it true that sheep eat little bushes?"

"Yes, that is true."

"Ah! I am glad!"

I did not understand why it was so important that sheep eat little bushes.

But the little prince added, "Do they also eat baobabs?" I pointed out to the little prince that baobabs were not little bushes. Even if he brought in all the elephants, they wouldn't eat a single baobab. The idea of all the elephants made the little prince laugh.

"We would have to put them one on top of the other," he said. He made a wise comment, "Before they grow so big, the baobabs start out by being little."

"That is correct," I said.

"But why do you want the sheep to eat the little baobabs?"

He answered me directly, "What are you talking about?"

I had to make a great mental effort to solve this problem without any help. There were, on the planet where the little prince lived, good seeds from good plants and bad seeds from bad plants. The seeds are hidden. They sleep deep in the earth, then the little seeds will stretch themselves. They will begin to push charming little leaves upward to the sun. When there is a bad plant, it should be destroyed as soon as possible.

There were some bad seeds on the little prince's planet. These were the seeds of the baobab. The ground of the planet was filled with them. Once a baobab takes root, it's a plant you can never get rid of if you realize it too late. It drills through planets with its roots. If the planet too small, and the baobabs are too many, they split it into pieces...

"It is a question of making a habit," the little prince said to me later. "When you've finished washing yourself in the morning, then it is time to think about your planet. Once they can be identified from the rosebushes, you must regularly pull up all the baobabs. Baobabs and rosebushes look similar in their early youth. It is very boring work, but very easy."

One day he said to me, "You should draw a picture for children where you live, so they can see exactly what all of this looks like. The problem of the baobabs should not be put off another day. That would be a disaster. I knew a planet where a lazy man lived. He ignored three little bushes..."

I have made a drawing of that planet. I don't like to talk like a moral person, but there are too few people who know the dangers of baobabs. I am making an exception this one time. "Children," I say clearly, "watch out for the baobabs!"

I have worked so hard on this drawing. The reason, my friends, is to warn people of hidden dangers. The lesson in my drawing is worth it. Perhaps you will ask me, "Why aren't other drawings as good as this baobab?" The answer is simple. I have tried, but I couldn't make it. When I made the drawing of the baobabs, I was very focused on drawing it because of its importance.

Chapter 6

Oh, little prince! Bit by bit, I came to understand the secrets of your sad little life... For a long time, you had found your only fun in looking at the sunset.

On the fourth day, I learned a new detail when you said to me, "I really love sunsets. Let's go look at a sunset."
"But we must wait," I said.
"Wait? For what?"
"For the sunset."
At first, you seemed to be surprised. Then, you laughed to yourself and said to me,
"I think that I am at home!"

Everybody knows that when it is noon in the United States, the sun is setting in France. If you could fly to France in a minute, you could see the sunset. For the little prince, watching the sunset is easy. He can see the sunset just by moving his chair a few steps.

"One day," you said to me, "I saw the sunset forty-four times!" And then, "When I am so sad, I love to look at the sunset..."
"Were you so sad at that time?" I asked, but the little prince didn't answer.

Chapter 7

On the fifth day, the secret of the little prince's life was shown to me again. Suddenly, he asked me after long and silent thought about his problem,

"If a sheep eats little bushes, does it eat flowers, too?"

"A sheep eats anything it finds," I answered.

"Even flowers that have thorns?"

"Yes, even flowers that have thorns."

"Then the thorns...what use are they?"

I did not know. At that moment, I was busy trying to fix my engine. I was very worried because my engine was seriously damaged and I had so little drinking water left.

"The thorns—what use are they?" the little prince asked again.

At that time, I was upset at a damaged bolt and I answered immediately, "The thorns are of no use at all."

"Oh!" After a silence, the little prince suddenly said,

"I don't believe you! Flowers are weak creatures. They are pure. They believe that their thorns are powerful weapons..."

I did not answer. The little prince said to me again, "You actually believe that the flowers..."

"Oh, no!" I cried. "No, no, no! I don't believe anything. I answered you with the first thing that came into my head. Don't you see? I am very busy with important work!"

He stared at me, shocked, "Important work!"

At that moment, I was bending down over my plane and my fingers were black with engine-oil.

 "You sound just like the grown-ups!" That made me a little sorry, but he went on,

"You mix everything up together... You confuse everything..." He was very angry.

"I know a red-faced gentleman who lives on a planet. He has never smelled a flower. He has never loved anyone. All day he says over and over, just like you, 'I am busy with important work!' But he is not a man. He is a mushroom!"

"A what?"

"A mushroom!" The little prince was now white with anger.

"For millions of years, flowers made thorns. For millions of years, sheep ate flowers. Is it not important to try to understand why the flowers have useless thorns? Doesn't the war with the sheep and the flowers matter? Is this not more important than a red-faced gentleman's numbers?"

"I know one flower that is special in the world. The flower grows only on my planet. But one little sheep can destroy it in one bite some morning. Oh! You think that is not important!"

His face turned from white to red as he continued, "If

someone loves a flower that is found only on one star, it makes him happy just to look at the stars. He can say to himself, 'Somewhere, my flower is there...' But if the sheep eats the flower, all his stars will be dark... You think that is not important!"

He could not say more. He cried. The night had fallen. I put down my tools. My hammer, bolt, thirst, and death were all stupid things to worry about. There was a little prince who needed to be comforted by someone.

I took him in my arms. I said to him,
"The flower that you love is not in danger. I will draw you a mask for your sheep. I will draw you a fence to put around your flower. I will..."
I did not know how I could reach him and go on hand in hand with him once more. The place of tears is a secret place.

Chapter 8

I got to know this flower better. On the little prince's planet, the flowers were very simple. They only needed a small space. One morning they would come out in the grass, and by night they would be gone peacefully.

One day, a new flower had come up, and the little prince had watched this small growing plant very closely. It was not like any other small sprouts on his planet. Maybe this was a new kind of baobab.

The plant soon stopped growing and began to get ready to flower. The little prince felt at once that something amazing would appear, but the flower was not ready for her beauty in her flower room. She chose her colors with the highest care. She dressed slowly. She checked her petals one by one. It was only in the full shine of her beauty that she wished to appear. Oh, yes! She was a charming creature! Her amazing makeup process continued for days and days.

One morning, she suddenly showed herself. She yawned and said,
 "Ah! I am hardly awake. Can you excuse me? My petals are still not perfect..."
But the little prince could not control his wonder,
"Oh! How beautiful you are!"

"Am I not?" the flower said. "I was born at the same time as the sun..."
The little prince could guess that she was too proud.

"I think it is time for breakfast," she added. "If you would think about my needs..."
The little prince went to look for fresh water. She quickly began to pain him with her self-love. The truth was, she was a little difficult to deal with.

One day, when she was speaking of her four thorns, she said to the little prince,
"Come on, tigers! I have four claws."
"There are no tigers on my planet," the little prince said.
"And tigers do not eat plants."
"I am not a plant," the flower replied.
"I'm sorry..."

"I am not at all afraid of tigers," she said, "but I am afraid of wind. Do you have a screen for me?"
"Afraid of the wind...that is bad luck for a plant," commented the little prince, and said to himself, "She is a very complex flower..."

"At night I want you to put me under a glass cup. It is very cold in the place

I came from..." She stopped speaking. She came from a seed, so she didn't know anything about any other worlds. She felt shy, so she coughed two or three times.

"The screen?"

"I was just going to look for it."

Then she forced her cough a little more so that he would feel guilty. Even though the little prince loved the flower deeply, he soon came to doubt her. He had taken her words seriously and it made him very unhappy.

"I should not have listened to her," he said to me one day. "No one should listen to flowers. Simply look at them and smell them. The story of claws upset me so much. I should only have pitied her."

He continued, "The fact is that I did not know how to understand anything! should have judged her by her actions, not her words. She gave off her smell and brightness to me. I should not have run away from her... Flowers are so unstable! I was too young to understand how to love her..."

144

Chapter 9

I believe that he left his planet with the help of a group of wild birds. On the morning of his departure, he put his planet in perfect order. He carefully cleaned out his active volcanoes. He used two active volcanoes for heating his breakfast.

He also had one dead volcano. But he said, "Who knows!" and cleaned out the dead volcano, too. If they are cleaned out, volcanoes burn slowly and steadily. On our Earth, we are surely too small to clean out our volcanoes. That is why they give us trouble.

The little prince also pulled up the last of the baobabs. He believed that he would never want to return. But on this last morning, all these jobs seemed very precious to him. When he watered the flower for the last time, he felt that he was very close to tears.

"Goodbye," he said to the flower. She didn't answer.
"Goodbye," he said again.
The flower coughed, but it was not because of a cold.
"I have been stupid," she said to him, at last. "I ask your forgiveness. Be happy..."

He was surprised by her kindness. He stood there, holding the glass cup, confused. He did not understand her sweetness.

"Of course I love you," the flower said to him. "It is my fault that you have not known it at all. But you...you have been just as foolish as me. Be happy... I don't need the glass cup anymore."

"But the wind..."

"My cold is not too bad... The cool night air will do me good. I am a flower."

"But the animals..."

"Well, I must accept two or three worms if I wish to see the butterflies. They are very beautiful. And if not the butterflies, who will come to me? You will be far away... I am also not at all afraid of the large animals. I have four thorns. Don't stay like this. Just go!"

She didn't want him to see her crying.

He carefully cleaned out his active volcanoes.

Chapter 10

He found himself near the small planets 325-330. He began visiting them. On the first planet, there was a king. He was seated on a royal chair.

"Ah! Here is a citizen," cried out the king when he saw the little prince coming. The little prince asked himself, "How could he know me?" He did not know how easy the world was for kings. To them, all men were citizens.

"Come close so that I may see you better," said the king.

The little prince looked everywhere to find a place to sit down, but the planet was filled with the king's clothes. So he stayed standing straight. The little prince was tired, and he yawned.

"It is not good manners to yawn in front of the king," he said to the little prince. "I order you to stop yawning."

"I can't stop myself," replied the little prince. "I had a long trip, and I have had no sleep..."

The king said, "I order you to yawn. I have not seen anyone yawning for some years. Yawn again!"

"That scares me... I can't yawn anymore..." the little prince said in a low voice.

"Hum! Hum!" replied the king.

"Then I—I order you sometimes to yawn and sometimes to—" He spoke with a bit of anger. Because his authority was so strong, he could not accept people who didn't obey.

He was an absolute king. But, because he was a very good man, he made his orders understandable. For example, "If I ordered a general to change himself into a bird, and if the general did not obey me, that would be my fault."

"May I sit down?" the little prince asked shyly.
"I order you to do so," the king answered. He gracefully gathered in the fold of his clothes. "But the little prince wondered... what could this king truly rule over on such a small planet?

"Sire," he said to him, "May I ask you a question..."
"I order you to ask me a question," the king said in a hurry.
"Sire, over what do you rule?"
"Over everything," answered the king simply.
"Over everything?"
The king pointed to his planet, the other planets, and all the stars.
"Over all that?" asked the little prince.
"Over all that," the king answered. His rule was universal.
"Do the stars obey you?"
"Sure they do," the king said. "They obey instantly."
That power was a wonder to the little prince. He would have been able to watch the sunset, not 44 times in a day, but 72 or even 100 or even 200 times, without ever having to move his chair.

He felt a bit sad as he remembered his little planet, so he asked the king a favor with courage, "I would like to see a sunset... Could you order the sun to set..."

"If I ordered a general to fly from one flower to another like a butterfly, and if the general did not follow the order, who would be in the wrong?" the king asked. "The general, or me?"

"You," said the little prince surely.
"Exactly. Each person should be required to do what each person can perform," the king went on. "First of all, accepted authority is based on reason. I have the power to order obedience because my orders are reasonable."

"Then what about my sunset?" the little prince reminded him.
"You shall have your sunset. I shall command it, but I shall wait until conditions are positive."
"When is that?" asked the little prince.
"Hmm, hmm!" the king looked at the big journal. "Hmm, hmm! That will be around twenty minutes to eight. You'll see how well they obey me!"

The little prince was already beginning to be a little bored. "I have nothing more to do here," he said to the king. "I shall go on my way again."
"Do not go," said the king. "Do not go. I will make you a leader in the government!"
"What kind of leader?"
"Minister of Justice!"

"But there is nobody here to judge!"

"Who knows?" the king said to him. "I have not yet perfectly made a tour of my kingdom."

"Oh, but I have looked already!" said the little prince. He turned around to give one more looking to the other side of the planet. There was nobody at all...

"Then you shall judge yourself," the king answered, "that is the most difficult thing of all. If you succeed in judging yourself, then you are really a wise man."

"Yes," said the little prince, "but I can judge myself anywhere."

"Hmm, hmm!" said the king. "There is an old rat on my planet. I hear him at night. You can judge this old rat. You can put him to death, but you will forgive him each time because he is the only one we have."

"I do not like to put anyone to death," replied the little prince. "Now I think I will go on my way."

"No," said the king.

But the little prince already finished getting ready for departure.

"If you give me a reasonable order, I can follow your order. For example, you can order me to be gone by the end of one minute."

The king made no answer. The little prince waited a moment. Then he went away.

"I make you my messenger for other planets," the king called out.

"The grown-ups are very strange," the little prince said to himself.

Chapter 11

On the second planet lived a
self-important man. "Ah! Ah!
I have a visitor who respects me!"
he cried out when he first saw the
little prince coming. Self-important
men always think that everyone
respects them.

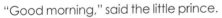

"Good morning," said the little prince.
"That is a strange hat you are wearing."
"It is a hat for greetings," the self-important
man replied.
"It is for raising in welcome when people clap for me.
However, nobody passes this way."
"Yes?" the little prince said.
"Clap your hands," the self-important man said to him.
The little prince clapped his hands. The self-important man
raised his hat in a simple greeting.
"This is more interesting than the visit to the king," the little
prince said to himself.

He began to clap his hands again. The self-important man
again raised his hat in simple greeting. After five minutes,
the little prince got tired of this game.
"How can I make your hat come down?" he asked.
But the self-important man did not hear him.

"Do you really respect me?" he demanded of the little prince.

"What does that mean, 'respect'?"

"To respect means that you think of me as the most handsome, the best-dressed, and the richest man on this planet."

"But you are the only man on your planet!"

"Please admire me just the same."

"I admire you," said the little prince, "but why does that interest you?" The little prince went away.

"The grown-ups are certainly very strange," he said to himself.

Chapter 12

On the next planet lived a drunk person.

"What are you doing there?"

He spoke to the drunk person who sat down among many empty and full bottles.

"I am drinking," replied the drunk person.

"Why are you drinking?" asked the little prince.

"So that I can forget," he replied.

"Forget what?" asked the little prince.

"Forget that I am ashamed," the drunk person dropped his head.

"Ashamed of what?" The little prince wanted to help him.

"Ashamed of drinking!" The drunk person silent after he said this.

"The grown-ups are certainly very, very odd," he said to himself as he continued on his journey.

Chapter 13

On the fourth planet, lived a businessman. This man was so busy he did not know of the little prince's arrival. "Good morning," the little prince said to him. "Your cigarette has gone out."

"3 and 2 make 5. 5 and 7 make 12. 12 and 3 make 15. Good morning. 15 and 7 make 22. 22 and 6 make 28. I have no time to light a cigarette again. 26 and 5 make 31. Phew! Then 501,622,731."

"Five hundred million of what?" asked the little prince.
"Eh? Are you still there? Five-hundred-and-one million...
I can't stop... I'm a person who's doing important work!
I don't interest myself with nonsense. Two and five make seven.
"Five-hundred-and-one million of what?" repeated the little prince. The businessman looked up.

"During the fifty-four years that I have lived on this planet, I have been disturbed only three times. The first time was when some crazy goose fell from somewhere. He made the most terrible noise, and I made four mistakes in my work. The second time, I was disturbed by pain in my leg muscle. The third time is now! Well... five-hundred-and-one million."

"Millions of what?" the little prince asked again.

The businessman realized that this question would continue until he got the answer.

"Millions of those little objects in the sky," he said.

"Flies?"

"Oh, no. Little twinkling objects."

"Bees?"

"Oh, no. Little golden objects."

"Ah! You mean the stars?"

"Yes, that's it. The stars."

"And what do you do with five-hundred millions of stars?"

"501,622,731. I am concerned with my important work."

"And what do you do with these stars?"

"What do I do with them?"

"Yes."

"Nothing. I own them."

"You own the stars?"

"Yes."

"But I have already seen a king who..."

"Kings do not own, they rule over."

"What good does it do you to own the stars?"

"It is good for making me rich."

"And what good does it do you to be rich?"

"I can buy more stars."

He still had some more questions.

"How is it possible to own the stars?"

"Who owns these stars?" the businessman replied angrily.

"I don't know. Nobody does."

"Then they belong to me because I was the first person to think of it."

"Is that all that is necessary?"

"Certainly. When you find a diamond that belongs to nobody, it is yours. When you discover an island that belongs to nobody, it is yours. I own the stars because nobody thought of owning them except me."

"Yes, that is true," said the little prince. "What do you do with them?"

"I manage them," replied the businessman. "I count them and recount them. It is difficult."

The little prince was still not satisfied. "If I owned a silk scarf,"

he said, "I could put it around my neck. If I owned a flower, I could pick that flower and take it away with me. But you cannot pick the stars up from heaven..."

"No, but I can put them in the bank."

"What does that mean?"

"That means that I write the number of my stars on a little paper and then I put this paper in the bank."

"And that is all?"

"That is enough," said the businessman.

"It's interesting," thought the little prince. "It is quite poetic, but it is not important." The little prince had very different ideas from the grown-ups about important things.

"I own a flower," he said to the businessman, "I water every day. I own three volcanoes, which I clean out every week. It is good for my volcanoes, and my flower, that I own them, but you are no use to the stars..."

The businessman had nothing to say for an answer. The little prince went away. "The grown-ups are certainly strange," he said to himself as he continued on his journey.

Chapter 14

The fifth planet was very strange. It was the smallest of all. There was only enough space for a street lamp and a lamplighter. The little prince could not understand why a street lamp was needed on such a small planet.

He said to himself, "Maybe this man is crazy, but he is not as crazy as the king, the self-important man, the businessman, and the drunk person, for he does normal work. When he lights his street lamp, he brings one more star to life. When he puts out his lamp, he sends the star to sleep. That is a beautiful job. It is beautiful, and it is truly useful."

He respectfully greeted the lamplighter. "Good morning. Why have you just put out your lamp?"

"Those are the orders," replied the lamplighter. "Good morning."

"What are the orders?"

"The orders are that I put out my lamp." He lighted his lamp again.

"Why have you just lighted it again?"

"Those are the orders," replied the lamplighter.

"I do not understand," said the little prince.

"There is nothing to understand," said the lamplighter. "Orders are orders." And he put out his lamp. Then he wiped his forehead with a handkerchief.

"I have a terrible job. In the old days, it was okay. I put the lamp out in the morning, and in the evening, I lighted it again. The other times I was free."

"And then the orders changed?"

"The orders didn't change," said the lamplighter. "That is the disaster!" From year to year, the planet has turned more quickly.

"Then what?" asked the little prince.

"Then the planet makes a turn every minute, and I don't have a single second for rest. Every minute, I have to light my lamp and put it out!"

"That is funny! A day continues for only one minute!"

"It is not funny at all!" said the lamplighter. "While we have been talking together a month has gone by."

"A month?"

"Yes, a month. Good evening."

He lighted his lamp again.

As the little prince watched him, he felt that he loved this lamplighter. He wanted to help his friend. "You know," he said, "I can tell you a way you can rest whenever you want to."

I follow a terrible profession.

"I always want to rest," said the lamplighter. The little prince went on,

"Your planet is so small that three steps are enough to go around it. If you walk slowly, you will always have sunshine, so you won't need to light the streetlamp."

"That doesn't help me," said the lamplighter. "The one thing I want is to sleep."

"Then you're unlucky," said the little prince.

"I am unlucky," said the lamplighter. He put out his lamp.

"That man would be hated by the king, by the drunk person, and by the businessman," said the little prince to himself. "He is the only one of them who is not silly. Perhaps it's because he works for others." He said to himself again, "That man is the only one who could be my friend. But his planet is too small. There is no room on it..."

He was sorry most of all to leave this planet on which he could see 1,400 sunsets every day.

Chapter 15

The sixth planet was much larger than the last one. There lived an old gentleman who wrote large books. "Oh, look! Here is an explorer!" he cried out to the little prince. The little prince sat down on the table. He had already traveled so much!

"Where do you come from?" the old gentleman said to him.

"What is that big book?" said the little prince. "What are you doing?"

"I am an earth scientist," said the old gentleman.

"What is an earth scientist?" asked the little prince.

"An earth scientist is a scientist who knows the location of all the seas, rivers, towns, and mountains."

"That is very interesting," said the little prince.

"This is a real job!" The little prince looked around at the planet. "Your planet is very beautiful," he said. "Does it have any oceans?"

"I couldn't tell you," said the scientist.

"Ah!" The little prince was disappointed. "Does it have any mountains?"

"I couldn't tell you that either," said the scientist.

"But you are an earth scientist!"

"Exactly," the scientist said. "But I am not an explorer. An earth scientist doesn't go out to count the towns, rivers, mountains, seas, and oceans. The earth scientist does not leave his desk."

The scientist went on, "So he receives the explorers in his study. He asks them questions and he writes down their travel stories. If he finds an interesting story, he tests that explorer's moral character."

"Why is that?"

"Because, if an explorer told lies, the earth science books would be fake books. A drunk person would cause trouble too."

"Why is that?" asked the little prince.

"Because drunk people see double. They would say there were two mountains, but actually, there was only one mountain."

"I know someone. Who would make a bad explorer," said the little prince.

"That is possible. When I meet a good explorer, I ask about his discovery."

"Does one go to see it?"

"No, that would be too difficult. But one asks the explorer for real data. For example, if an explorer discovers a large mountain, I demand large stones from that mountain."

The earth scientist suddenly shouted. "But you, you come from far away! You are an explorer! Tell me about your planet!"

Having opened his big book, the scientist sharpened his pencil. He put it down first in pencil before putting in ink.

"Well?" said the scientist.

"Oh, where I live," said the little prince, "Everything is small. I have three volcanoes. Two volcanoes are active, and the other one is not. I also have a flower."

"We do not write about flowers," said the scientist.

"Why is that?"

"Because they are short life span," said the scientist.

"What does that mean, 'short life span'?"

"The books of earth science are the most important books of all." said the scientist. "They never become old-fashioned. We write of things that don't change."

"But dead volcanoes may come to life again," the little prince stopped. "What does that mean, 'short life span'?"

"Whether volcanoes are alive or not, it makes no difference to us," said the earth scientist.

"But what does that mean, 'short life span'?" repeated the little prince.

"It means, 'that is quick to disappear.'"

"Does my flower have a short lifespan?"

"Certainly, it is."

"My flower is short life span," the little prince said to himself, and I have left her on my planet, all alone!" That was his first time to feel sorry, but he took courage once more.

"What place do I visit now?" he asked.

"The planet Earth," the scientist said.

The little prince went away, thinking of his flower.

Chapter 16

The seventh planet was the Earth. The Earth is a special planet! There are 111 kings, 7000 earth scientists, 900,000 businessmen, 7,500,000 drunks people, 311,000,000 self-important men, which means about 2,000,000,000 grown-ups.

To give you an idea of the size of the Earth, I will tell you that the Earth needed 462,511 lamplighters for the street lamps. When seen from a little distance, the movements of this group would look like a ballet performance.

First, there would be the lighting of the lamps of New Zealand and Australia, next, the lamplighters of China and Siberia would enter in the dance. After that, there would be the turn of the lamps of Russia and the Indies, and then those of Africa and Europe. Then there would be those of South America, then those of North America. They would never make a mistake in entering on the stage.

It would be amazing. There were two men. One was at the North Pole and the other one was at the South Pole. These two would be busy only twice a year.

Chapter 17

When one wishes to try to be smart, he sometimes goes a little far from the truth. I was not fully honest with what I told you about the lamplighters. Men occupy a very small place on Earth. If the 2,000,000,000 people on its surface stood upright, they could easily fit into a single public square.

The grown-ups will not believe you when you tell them that. They believe that they fill a great deal of space. You should advise them to do their own counting, but do not waste your time on this extra task. Just trust me.

When the little prince arrived on the Earth, he couldn't find any people. He was afraid he had come to the wrong planet. At that time, he saw a golden ring moving on the sand.
"Good evening," said the little prince.
"Good evening," said the snake.
"What is this planet?" asked the little prince.
"This is the Earth," the snake answered.
"Ah! Then there are no people on the Earth?"
"This is the African desert. There are no people in the desert. The Earth is large," said the snake.

The little prince sat down on a stone and raised his eyes to the sky.
"Why are the stars bright?" he said, "Maybe they show us

the way to find our own stars. Look at my planet. It is right there above us!"

"It is beautiful," the snake said. "What has brought you here?"

"I had some trouble with a flower," said the little prince.

"Ah!" said the snake.

They were both silent.

"Where are the men?" the little prince asked the snake again. "It is a little lonely in the desert..."

"It is also lonely among men," the snake said. The little prince looked at him for a long time.

"You are a funny animal," he said. "You are so thin..."

"But I am so powerful," said the snake.

The little prince smiled. "You are not very powerful. You don't even have any feet."

"I can carry you to far distances," said the snake.

He twisted himself around the little prince's foot, "If I touch someone, I can send him back to where he came from."

The snake spoke again, "But you are pure and true, and you come from a star. You move me to pity. I can help you, someday, if you grow too homesick. I can..."

"Oh! I understand you very well," said the little prince. "But why do you always speak in a puzzle?"

"I can solve all puzzles." said the snake.

Chapter 18

The little prince crossed the desert and met a flower. It was a flower with three petals.

"Good morning," said the little prince.

"Good morning," said the flower.

"Where are the men?" the little prince asked.

"Men?" she echoed. "I saw them several years ago, but I never know where to find them. They have no roots, which makes their lives very difficult."

"Goodbye," said the little prince.

"Goodbye," said the flower.

Chapter 19

After that, the little prince climbed a high mountain. The only mountains he had ever known were his three little volcanoes.

"From the top of a mountain, I shall be able to see the whole planet with one look," he said to himself. But he saw nothing except the pointed tops of rocks.

"Good morning," he said.

"Good morning, Good morning, Good morning," answered the echo.

"Who are you?" said the little prince.

"Who are you, Who are you, Who are you?" answered the echo.

"Be my friend. I am all alone," he said.

"I am all alone, all alone, all alone," answered the echo.

"What a strange planet!" he thought. "It is really dry and pointed and tough. The people have no creativity. They just repeat whatever I say. My flower was always the first to speak..."

Chapter 20

After walking for a long time through the sand, the little prince came upon a road. All roads lead to the houses of men.

"Good morning," he said, standing before a garden.
"Good morning," said the roses. They all looked like the little prince's flower.
"Who are you?" he asked quickly.
"We are roses," the roses said.

He was overcome with sadness because of what his flower said. She told him, "I am the only one of my kind in all the world," but here were over five thousand roses. "She would be very upset," he said to himself, "if she could see that, she would pretend that she was dying, and I would pretend that I was nursing her back to life. If I did not do that, she would really allow herself to die..."

Then he went on, "I thought that I was rich, with a unique flower, but all I had was a common rose. I had a common rose and three volcanoes. That doesn't make me a great prince..." He lay down in the grass and cried.

Chapter 21

At that time, the fox came out. "Good morning," said the fox.

"Good morning," the little prince said kindly. But when he turned around, he saw nothing.

"I am right here," the voice said, "under the apple tree."

"Who are you? You are very pretty," asked the little prince.

"I am a fox," the fox said.

"Come and play with me," suggested the little prince. "I am very unhappy."

"I cannot play with you," the fox said. "I am wild."

"Ah! Sorry," said the little prince. But he added, "What does that mean, 'wild'?"

"It means 'not tamed.'"

And he lay down in the grass and cried.

"You do not live here," said the fox. "What are you looking for?"

"I am looking for men," said the little prince. "What does that mean, 'tame'?"

"Men," said the fox. "They have guns and they hunt. They also raise chickens."

"Are you looking for chickens?"

"No," said the little prince. "I am looking for friends. What does that mean, 'tame'?"

"It means 'to be able to make relationships'," said the fox.
"Make a relationship?"
"Just that," said the fox.

"To me, you are a little boy who is just like a hundred thousand other little boys. To you, I am a fox like a hundred thousand other foxes. But if you tame me, then we shall need each other. We will be unique to each other in all the world.
"I understand," said the little prince. "There is a flower on my planet. I think that she has tamed me."
"It is possible... What? On another planet?" said the fox.
"Yes."
"Are there hunters on that planet?"
"No."
"Ah, that is interesting! Are there chickens?"
"No."
"Nothing is perfect," the fox said with disappointment.

After a while, the fox said,"My life is very simple. I hunt chickens. Men hunt me. That's all. I am a little bored. But if you tame me, it will be like sunshine in my life. I will know the sound of your footsteps. They will be like music. If I hear the sound of your feet, I will come out of my shelter."

"And look at the golden grain fields over there. I do not eat bread. Wheat is of no use to me. The wheat fields have nothing to say to me. But you have golden hair. If you tamed me, the grain would make me think of you."

The fox looked at the little prince for a long time. "Please! Tame me!" the fox said.

"I want to very much, but I don't have much time. I have friends to see, and a great many things to understand."

"Men don't have time anymore to understand anything. They buy everything from shops, but there is no shop selling friendships. So they don't have friends. If you want a friend, tame me..." said the fox.

"What must I do to tame you?" asked the little prince.

"You must be very patient," said the fox. "First, you will sit down a little bit away from me. I will look at you out of the side of my eye and you will say nothing. But you will sit a little closer to me, every day..."

The next day the little prince came back.

"It would have been better to come back at the same hour," said the fox. "For example, if you come at four o'clock, then I shall begin to be happy at three o'clock. But, if you come at just any time, I would never know when my heart would be ready to greet you..."

"That's why we have to make a special day..."

"What is a special day?" asked the little prince.

"Those actions are often ignored," said the fox. "A special day is that one day different from other days. For example, every Thursday, hunters dance with the village girls. So Thursday is a wonderful day for me! I can walk everywhere freely. But if the hunters danced at any time, every day would be like every other day."

So the little prince tamed the fox, and when he had to leave...

"Ah," said the fox, "I shall cry."

"It is your fault," said the little prince. "I never wished you any kind of pain."

"Yes, that's right," said the fox.

"But now you are going to cry!" said the little prince.

"Yes, that's right," said the fox.

"Then it was not good for you at all!"

"It has been good for me," said the fox. "Go and look again at the roses. You will under-stand that your rose is unique in all the world.

"For example, if you come at four o'clock in the afternoon, then at three o'clock I shall begin to be happy."

Then come back to say goodbye to me, and I will give you a secret."

The little prince went to the roses.
"You are not like my rose," he said. "You are nothing now. No one has tamed you. You are roses like a hundred thousand other roses." The roses were very much ashamed. "You are beautiful, but you are empty," he went on. "No one could die for you, but my rose is more important than all the hundreds of you other roses. Because I have watered her, put her under the glass cup, covered her with the screen, and killed the worms for her. I have listened to everything she said, because she is my rose."

He went back to meet the fox. "Goodbye," he said.
"Goodbye," said the fox. "Now, here is my secret: The most important things cannot be seen with the eye."
"The most important things cannot be seen with the eye," the little prince repeated so that he would be sure to remember.
"You spent time on your rose, and that makes your rose so important."
"I have spent time on my rose..." said the little prince.
"You have become responsible for your rose..."
"I am responsible for my rose," the little prince repeated so that he would be sure to remember.

Chapter 22

"Good morning," said the little prince.

"Good morning," said the railway switchman.

"What do you do here?" the little prince asked.

"I send off the trains to the right or the left," said the switch-man.

A lighted express train rushed by with a loud sound like thunder.

"They are in a great hurry," said the little prince. "What are they looking for?"

"Even the train driver doesn't know that," said the switchman.

And a second lighted express train rushed by.

"Are they coming back already?" asked the little prince.

"These are not the same ones," said the switchman.

"It's a different train."

They heard the loud sound of thunder. A third fully lighted express train rushed by.

"Are they following the first travelers?" asked the littleprince.

"They are following nothing at all," said the switchman.

"They are asleep inside. Only the children are awake, playing with the windows."

"Only the children know what they are looking for," said the little prince.

"They are lucky," the switchman said.

Chapter 23

"Good morning," said the little prince.
"Good morning," said the seller.

There was a seller who sold capsules. If you eat one capsule a week, you will have no need to drink water.
"Why are you selling those?" asked the little prince.
"Because they save time," said the seller.
"You will save fifty-three minutes each week with these capsules."
"What could I do with those fifty-three minutes?"
"Anything you like..."
"If I had fifty-three minutes, I would walk to a spring of fresh water," said the little prince to himself.

Chapter 24

It was now the eighth day since my accident. I had listened to the story of the seller as I was drinking the last drop of my water.

"Ah, your stories are very interesting," I said to the little prince. "My plane is still not working and I have no more water to drink. I would be happy if I could walk toward a spring of fresh water!"

"My friend the fox..." the little prince said to me.
"My dear little man, this is not the time to talk about the fox!"
"Why not?"
"Because I am about to die of thirst..."
He answered me, "Even if we are about to die, it is good that we were friends..."

"He doesn't understand the danger of our situation," I said to myself. "He has never been thirsty." He looked at me slowly and answered my thought,
"I am thirsty, too. Let us look for a well..."
It is strange to search for a well in the desert, but we started walking.

When we had walked for some hours, the darkness fell and the stars began to come out.

Thirst had made me a little hot. Then I suddenly remembered his last words,

"Are you thirsty too?" I asked.

But he didn't answer my question. He only said to me,

"Water may also be good for the heart..."

I did not understand this answer, but I said nothing.

He was tired. He sat down. He spoke again,

"The stars are beautiful because of a flower that cannot be seen."

I replied, "Yes, that's right." I looked across the hills of sand without saying anything.

"The desert is beautiful," the little prince said.

And that was true. I have always loved the desert.

"What makes the desert beautiful," said the little prince: "a hidden well is making the desert beautiful."

I was surprised by a sudden understanding of the desert. The desert is beautiful because there is water one cannot see.

When I was a little boy, I lived in an old house. There had been a story of hidden treasure under the house. This story cast magic on that house.

"Yes," I said to the little prince. "The house, the stars, the desert... their beauty is something that can't be seen!"

"I am glad," he said, "that you agree with my fox."

As the little prince fell asleep, I took him in my arms and began to walk once more. It seemed to me that I was

carrying a treasure that would easily break. I looked at his forehead, his closed eyes, and his hair in the moonlight.
I said to myself,
"What I see here is nothing but a shell. The most important things can't be seen..."

The little prince smiled. I said to myself,
"What touches my heart about this little prince who is sleeping, is his loyal heart for his flower."
I felt that he was weak. I needed to protect him. He looked like he would go out like a fire. We found water in the morning.

Chapter 25

"Men go by express trains," said the little prince. "But they don't know what they are looking for. They are busy, but they are still in the same place." He added, "It is more trouble than it's worth..."

The well we found was different from the wells in the desert. This well was like a well in a village, but there was no village here and I thought I must be dreaming...

"It is strange," I said to the little prince. "Everything is ready for use..."

He laughed, touched the rope, and pulled it. Then there was a sound of an old wheel, like an old windmill that hadn't moved in a long time.

"Do you hear?" said the little prince. "We have awakened the well and it is singing..."

I did not want him to tire himself. "Leave this rope to me," I said. "It's too heavy for you."

I pulled the bucket slowly to the edge of the well. The well's song still rang in my ears, and I could see the sunlight dancing on the water.

"I am thirsty for this water," said the little prince. "Give me some of it to drink..."

I understood what he had been looking for. He drank the water and his eyes closed. It was as sweet as festival food.

This water was certainly different from other water. This water tasted like it came from under the stars, from the song of the well. It was good for the heart, like a gift. When I was a little boy, the lights of the Christmas tree, the Christmas songs, and the smiling faces made the gifts of Christmas special.

"The men may raise five thousand roses in the garden, but they do not find what they are looking for. It could be found in one single rose or in a little water," said the little prince.

"Yes, that is true," I said.

And the little prince added,

"The eyes are useless. You must look with the heart..."

I drank the water. At sunrise, the sand was the color of honey. That honey color was making me happy too. What then brought me this sense of deep sadness?

"You must keep your promise," said the little prince as he sat down beside me.

"What promise?"

"You know... a mask for my sheep... I am responsible for this flower..."

I took out my drawings from my pocket. The little prince looked them over and laughed as he said, "Your baobabs look a little like cabbages. Your fox... his ears are too pointy and they are too long." He laughed again.

"You are not fair, little prince," I said. "I don't know how to draw anything except boa snakes."

"Oh, that will be alright," he said, "children understand."

Then I made a pencil sketch of a mask. When I gave it to him, I felt sad.

"You have plans that I do not know about," I said.

But he did not answer me. He said to me,

"You know... tomorrow will be one year since I came to earth."

Then after a moment, he went on, "I came down very near here." His face turned red.

I don't know why I had a strange sense of sadness, but one question came to my mind, "So, when you first met me, were you on your way back to where you came from?"

The little prince's face turned red again.

I added, "Perhaps it was because of the anniversary?"

The little prince's face turned red once more. He never answered questions, but I knew the red face meant "Yes."

"Ah," I said to him, "I'm a little scared..."

He stopped me. "Now, you must work. You must return to your plane. I will be waiting for you here. Come back tomorrow evening..."

I felt uncomfortable.

Chapter 26

Beside the well, there was an old stone wall. When I came back from my work, I saw my little prince sitting on top of a wall from some distance away. I heard him say, "This is not the exact place." Another voice must have answered him, for he replied to it,

"Now, go away, I want to get down from the wall."

"Yes, yes! It is the right day, but this is not the place."

I continued my walk to the wall. The little prince replied once again,

"Exactly. You will see my footprint in the sand. You have nothing to do but wait for me there. I will be there tonight."
I still saw nothing. After a moment, the little prince said again,

"You have good poison? You are sure that it will not make me hurt for too long?"
I stopped. My heart was broken, but I still did not understand.
"Now go away," said the little prince. "I want to get down from the wall."

I dropped my eyes to the foot of the wall. There was a

yellow snake that could end your life in thirty seconds. That snake was facing the little prince in front of me. I took a step back and I pulled my gun out of my pocket. However, I made some noise and the yellow snake disappeared slowly among the stones. I reached the wall and caught my little man in my arms. His face was white as snow.

"Why are you talking with snakes?" I untied the golden scarf and gave him some water to drink.

Now I did not ask him any more questions. He looked at me very seriously and put his arms around my neck. I felt his heart beating weakly.

"I am glad that you have fixed your plane," he said. "Now you can go back home."
"How do you know that?" I was just coming to tell him that my work had been successful. He made no answer to my question, but he said,
"I am also going back home today..."
Then, sadly, he said, "It is very far away... It is much more difficult."
I knew that something was happening. I was holding him close in my arms, but it seemed to me that he was falling into a deep place and I couldn't catch him...

His look was very serious, like someone lost far away.

"I have your sheep. I have the sheep's box. I have the mask..." I waited for a long time. I could see that he was getting better little by little.

"Dear little man," I said to him, "You are afraid..."

He was afraid, but he laughed lightly. "I shall be much more afraid this evening..."

Once again, I felt frozen. I knew that I could not hear that laughter any more.

"Little man," I said, "I want to hear you laugh again."

But he said to me,

"Tonight, it will be a year... My star can be found right above the place where I dropped off."

"Little man," I said, "tell me that it is only a bad dream..."

But he did not answer me. He said to me,

"Important things cannot be seen..."

"Yes, I know..."

"It is just like a flower. If you love a flower that lives on a star, it is sweet to look at the sky at night."

"Yes, I know..."

"It is just like water. Because of the well and the rope, what you gave me to drink was like music. You remember how good it was."

"Yes, I know..."

"At night you will look up at the stars. Everything on my star is so small that you can't find my star. But my star will be just one of the stars for you. You will love to watch all the stars in the heavens..."

He laughed again.

"Ah, little prince! I love to hear that laughter!"

"That is my present. It was like when we drank the water..."

"What are you trying to say?"

"All men have the stars," he answered, "but they are not the same for different people. For travelers, the stars are guides, and for others, stars are just little lights in the sky. For scientists, the stars are problems. For my businessman, stars are money."

"You will have the stars in a special way."

"What are you trying to say?"

"In one of the stars, I shall be living. In one of them, I shall be laughing. When you look at the sky at night, all the stars will be laughing. You will have stars that can laugh!"

He laughed again. "You will always be my friend. You will want to laugh with me. You will sometimes open your window for that joy... and your friends will be surprised to see you laughing at the sky. Then you will say to them, 'Yes, the stars always make me laugh!' They will think you are crazy." he laughed again.

"I had given you a great number of little bells that knew how to laugh..." He laughed again.

Then he quickly became serious.

"Tonight... you know... Do not come."

"I shall not leave you," I said.

"I shall look like I'm in pain. I shall look I am dying. Do not come to see that. It will be more trouble than it's worth..."
"I shall not leave you."

He was worried. "The snake must not bite you. Snakes are unkind creatures. This one might bite you just for fun..."
"I shall not leave you." However, a thought came to comfort him.
"It is true that they have no more poison for a second bite."

That night I did not see him go on his way. He got away from me without any noise. When I succeeded in catching up, he was walking along with a steady step. He said to me simply, "Ah! You are there..."
And he took me by the hand.
"It was wrong of you to come. You will be hurt. I shall look as if I were dead, but that will not be true..."
I said nothing.

And he sat down, because he was afraid.

"You know... it is too far. I cannot carry this body. It is too heavy."

I said nothing.

"It will be like an old empty shell. There is nothing sad about old shells..."

I said nothing.

He said once more, "You know, it will be very nice. When I shall look at the stars, they will be wells with a sound."

I said nothing.

"That will be so interesting! You will have five hundred million little bells and I shall have five hundred million springs of fresh water..." He too said nothing more, because he was crying...

"Here it is."

He sat down because he was afraid. Then he said,

"You know... my flower... I am responsible for her and she is so weak! She is so simple! She has four thorns to protect herself against all the world..."

I also sat down because I couldn't stand up any longer.

"That is all..." He paused a little. Then he got up and he took one step. I could not move. There was nothing but a flash of yellow close to his foot. He did not cry out. He fell as gently as a tree falls. There was not even any sound because of the sand.

Chapter 27

That was six years ago... I have never told this story until now. My friends were glad to see me alive again. I was sad, but I told them, "I am tired." Now my sadness is comforted a little. I know that he did go back to his planet because I did not find his body. At night I love to listen to the stars. It is like five hundred million little bells...

However, there is one strange thing... when I drew the mask for the little prince, I forgot to draw the rope for the sheep. He would never have been able to put the mask on his sheep. What is happening now on his planet? Perhaps the sheep has eaten the flower...

I say to myself, "Certainly not! The little prince shuts his flower under her glass cup every night." Then the little bells laughed.

At another time I say to myself, "What if he forgot the glass cup or the sheep got out without any noise in the night..." Then the little bells are changed to tears...

Here is a great mystery. For you and for me who love the little prince, the whole universe depends on whether the sheep ate the flower or not. Look up at the sky. Ask yourselves. Is it yes or no? Has the sheep eaten the flower? You will see how everything changes... Grown-ups will never understand that this is a matter of so much importance!

This is the loveliest and saddest landscape in the world. I drew it again so you will remember. It is here that the little prince appeared on Earth and disappeared.
Be sure to look at this carefully, in case you travel someday to the African desert. Then, if a little man appears who has golden hair, you will know who he is. If this happens, please let me know that he came back.

He fell as gently as a tree falls.

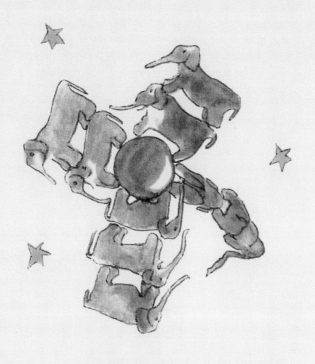

Level 4는 원문의 문장을 이해할 수 있도록
단어와 구문을 쉽게 만들었어요.
Level 4를 읽고 원문인 Level 5를 읽으면
원문의 어려운 단어들도 자연스럽게 유추할 수 있습니다.

In the Level 4 book, words and word orders are easier than
the original copy.
If you read the Level 4 book, before reading the Level 5 book, you can infer
difficult words that you encounter in the original copy.

THE ORIGINAL TEXT

The grown-ups' response, this time, was to advise me to lay aside my drawings of boa constrictors, whether from the inside or the outside, and devote myself instead to geography, history, arithmetic, and grammar. That is why, at the age of six, I gave up what might have been a magnificent career as a painter. I had been disheartened by the failure of my Drawing Number One and my Drawing Number Two. Grown-ups never understand anything by themselves, and it is tiresome for children to be always and forever explaining things to them.

LEVEL 4

The grown-ups advised me this time,
"Stop drawing boa snakes. Focus on geography, history, and grammar."
This is why I gave up being a great painter at six years old. I had been disappointed by the failure of drawing Number one and two. Grown-ups never understand anything by themselves. It's tiring for children to explain everything to grown-ups.

The Little Prince
LEVEL 4 ◼◼◼◼

어린왕자 레벨4

Chapter 1

Once when I was six years old, I saw a fantastic picture in a book called 'True Stories from Nature' about the jungle forest. It was a picture of a Boa snake in the act of eating an animal. Here is a copy of the drawing.

In the book, it said,

"Boa snakes eat animals without biting them. After that, they cannot move and will sleep for six months until the next hunt."

I carefully studied that book, True Stories from Nature. After some work with a pencil, I succeeded in making my first drawing. My Drawing Number One looked like this:

first drawing

I showed my drawing to the grown-ups.

"Does this drawing scare you?" I asked them.

They answered:

"Scared? Why should anyone be scared of a hat?"

My drawing was not a picture of a hat. It was a picture of a boa snake with an elephant in its body, but the grown-ups were not able to understand it. So I made another drawing. I drew the inside of the boa snake. Now the grown-ups were able to understand it clearly. They always need an explanation. My Drawing Number Two looked like this:

drawing No.2

The grown-ups advised me this time, "Stop drawing boa snakes. Focus on Geography, History, and Grammar instead." That is why I gave up being a great painter at six years old. I had been disappointed by the failure of my Drawing Number One and Two. Grown-ups never understand anything by themselves. It's tiring for children to explain everything to grown-ups.

I chose another job. I learned to pilot airplanes. I have flown all over the world. It is true that Geography has been very useful to me. I can distinguish China from Arizona very quickly. If I get lost at night, this knowledge is useful. During my lifetime, I have met many people who are concerned about important matters. I have seen them closely, and that hasn't changed my opinion of them much.

Whenever I met a very clear-sighted person, I tried the test of showing him my Drawing Number One. I have always kept my Drawing Number One. I would try to find out if he had real understanding. But, whoever it was, he, or she, would always say:

"That is a hat."

Then I would never talk to that person about boa snakes, or jungle forests, or stars. I would lower myself to his level. I would talk to him about card games, golf, politics, and neckties. And the grown-up would be happy to have met such a sensible man.

Chapter 2

So, I lived my life alone, with no one to really talk to, until I had an accident in the Desert of Sahara, six years ago.

Something was broken in my engine. And I had neither a mechanic nor any passengers. I had to make repairs by myself. I decided to try a difficult repair by myself. It was a question of life or death for me: I only had drinking water to last a week.

The first night, I went to sleep on the sand, I was a thousand miles from any human town. I was more alone than a broken ship's sailor on a piece of wood in the ocean. So, you can imagine my surprise at sunrise. I was awakened by a strange little voice. It said:

"If you please, draw me a sheep!"

"What?"

"Draw me a sheep!"

I jumped to my feet, completely shocked. I blinked my eyes hard. I looked carefully all around me. And I saw the most strange small person standing there looking at me with great seriousness. You can see here the best drawing of that person that I made later.

But my drawing is very much less charming than its model.

Here you may see the best portrait that, later, I was able to make of him.

However, that is not my fault. The grown-ups discouraged me in my dream of being a painter when I was six years old. And I never learned to draw anything, except boa snakes.

Now I looked at this unexpected appearance with my eyes almost jumping out of my head in surprise. Remember, I had crashed in the desert a thousand miles from any human area.

And yet my little man seemed to be neither lost nor unsure among the sands. he was not shocked from tiredness or hunger or thirst or fear. Nothing about him gave any suggestion of a child lost in the desert, a thousand miles from any human town.

At last, when I was able to speak, I said to him:

"What are you doing here?"

And in reply he repeated, very slowly, as if he were speaking of a matter of great importance:

"If you please—draw me a sheep..."

When a mystery is too strong, nobody can disobey. Crazy as it might seem to me, a thousand miles from any human town and in danger of death, I took a sheet of paper and a pen from my pocket.

But then I remembered how my studies had been focused on Geography, History, and Grammar, so I told the little man (in an upset tone)that I did not know how to draw. He answered me:

"That doesn't matter. Draw me a sheep..."

But I had never drawn a sheep, so I drew him one of the two pictures I often drew. It was a picture of the boa snake from the outside.

And I was shocked to hear the little boy react by saying, "No, no! I do not want an elephant inside a boa snake. A boa snake is a very dangerous animal and an elephant is very heavy. Where I live, everything is very small. What I need is a sheep. Draw me a sheep."

So then I made a drawing. He looked at it carefully, then he said:

"No. This sheep is already very sickly. Make me another

one." So I made another drawing. My friend smiled gently and kindly.

"Look at this," he said, "This is not a sheep. This is a ram. It has horns."

So then I made my drawing over again, but it was rejected too, just like the others. "This one is too old."

By this time my patience was gone, because I was in a hurry to repair my engine. So I tossed aside his drawing and I threw him an explanation.

"This is his box. The sheep you want is inside."

I was very surprised to see the face of my young judge become brighter:

"That is exactly the way I wanted it! Do you think that this sheep will have a great deal of grass?"

"Why?"

"Because where I live everything is very small..."

"There will be enough grass for him," I said. "It is a very small sheep that I have given you."

He looked at the drawing.

"Not so small that—Look! He has gone to sleep..."

And that is how I made friends with the little prince.

Chapter 3

It took a long time to learn where he came from. The little prince, who asked me so many questions, but he never seemed to hear what I asked him. It was from words dropped by chance. Little by little, everything was known to me.

For example, the first time he saw my airplane, he asked me:

"What is that thing?"

"That is not a thing. It flies. It is an airplane. It is my airplane." (I will not draw my airplane; that would be very difficult for me.) I was proud to let him know that I could fly.

He cried out, then: "What! You dropped down from the sky?"

"Yes," I answered quietly.

"Oh! That is funny!" And the little prince broke into lovely laughter. The sound of his laughter annoyed me very much. I wanted my unlucky situation to be taken seriously.

Then he added: "So you, too, come from the sky! Which is your planet?"

At that moment, I caught the light of his hard-to-understand presence. And I demanded suddenly:

"Do you come from another planet?" But he did not reply.

He tossed his head gently, without taking his eyes from my plane.

"It is true that on that you can't have come from very far away..." And he sank into a daydream, for a long time. Then, taking my sheep out of his pocket, he meditated on his treasure. You can imagine how my curiosity was awakened by this half-confidence about the "other planets." I tried very hard to find out more about this subject.

"My little man, where do you come from? What is this 'where I live,' of which you speak? Where do you want to take your sheep?" After thinking in silence, he answered:

"The box you have given me, at night he can use as his house."

"That is so. And if you are good, I will also give you a string so that you can tie him up during the day. I will also give you a post to tie him to."

But the little prince seemed shocked by this offer:

"Tie him! What an odd idea!"

"But if you don't tie him," I said, "he will go off somewhere and get lost."

My friend broke into another loud laugh:

"But where do you think he would go?"

"Anywhere. Straight ahead of him." Then the little prince said, seriously:

"That doesn't matter. On my planet, everything is so small!" And, with a little bit of sadness, he added:

"Straight ahead, nobody can go very far..."

Chapter 4

Thus I had learned a second fact of great importance. The planet the little prince came from was only just a little larger than a house! But that did not really surprise me much. I knew very well the great planets, like the Earth, Jupiter, Mars, and Venus, to which we have given names. And there are also hundreds of planets, and some of them are so small. It is hard to see them through a telescope.

When an astronomer discovers one of these, he does not give it a name. But he only gives it a number, like "Asteroid 325." I have good reason to believe that the little prince came from the asteroid known as B-612.

This asteroid has been seen through a telescope in 1909 by a Turkish astronomer. The astronomer had presented it to the IAC(International Astronomical Congress). He gave a great presentation, but he was in Turkish costume. Nobody would believe what he said. Grown-ups are like that...

Fortunately, Asteroid B-612 became more popular. A Turkish leader with absolute power made a law. The law was that his subjects had to change to European costume. (If they didn't obey, they would die.) So in 1920, the astronomer gave his presentation over again, dressed with excellent style and grace. And this time everybody accepted his report.

If I have told you these details about the asteroid and made a note of its number for you, it is because of the grown-ups and their ways. When you tell them that you have made a new friend, they never ask you any questions about important matters. "What does his voice sound like? What games does he love best? Does he collect butterflies?" Instead, they demand: "How old is he? How many brothers has he? How much does he weigh? How much money does his father make?" Only from these numbers do they think they have learned anything about him.

If you were to say to the grown-ups: "I saw a beautiful house made of rosy brick with flowerpots in the windows," they would not be able to get any idea of that house at all. You would have to say to them: "I saw a house that cost 20,000 dollars." Then, they would exclaim: "Oh, what a pretty house that is!"

You might say to them: "The fact that the little prince existed is that he was charming, that he laughed, and that he was looking for a sheep. If anybody wants a sheep, that shows that he exists." What's the use of telling them so? They would move their shoulders up and down and treat you like a child.

But if you said to them: "The planet he came from is Asteroid B-612," then they would be sure, and make you feel peaceful with their questions. They are like that. You must not blame them. Children should always show great patience to grown-up people. But yes, numbers don't really matter to us who really understand life.

I wish I could have begun this story in the style of the fairytales. I should have liked to say: "Once upon a time there was a little prince who lived on a planet that was just only bigger than himself, and he had need of a sheep..." To those who understand life, that would have given a much greater feeling of truth to my story. I do not want anyone to read my book casually.

I have felt too much sorrow in writing down these memories. Six years have already passed since my friend went away from me with his sheep. If I try to describe him here, it's to make sure that I shall not forget him. To forget a friend is sad. And if I forget him, I may become like the grown-ups who are interested in numbers...

For this purpose, I have bought a box of paints and some pencils. It is hard to start drawing again at my age. I have never made any pictures except the boa snake from the outside and the inside of the boa snake since I was six.

I shall try to make human drawings as true as possible, but I am not at all sure if I will have success. One drawing goes all right, and another is not same as its subject. I make some errors in the little prince's height: in one place he is too tall and in another too short. And I feel some doubt about his clothing color. So I proceed step by step, doing the best I can, sometimes good, sometimes bad, and hopefully average.

I may make mistakes in more important details as well. But that is something that will not be my fault. My friend never explained anything to me. He thought that I was like himself. But sadly, I do not know how to see sheep through the walls of boxes. Perhaps I am a little like the grownups. I have grown old.

The little prince standing on asteroids B612.

Chapter 5

As each day passed, I would learn something about the little prince's planet, his departure from his planet, and his journey. The information would come very slowly. Sometimes, it would fall from his thoughts. This was how I learned about the problem of the baobabs on the third day. This time, once more, I had the sheep to thank for it.

The little prince asked me suddenly—as if he was captured by a serious doubt—"It is true, isn't it, that sheep eat little bushes?"

"Yes, that is true."

"Ah! I am glad!"

I did not understand why it was so important that sheep eat little bushes.

But the little prince added: "And after that, they also eat baobabs?"

I pointed out to the little prince that baobabs were not little bushes. Baobabs, on the other hand, are trees as big as a castle. Even if he brought a whole herd of elephants, they would not be able to eat a single baobab.

The idea of the herd of elephants made the little prince laugh. "We would have to put them one on top of the other," he said.

But he made a wise comment:

"Before they grow so big, the baobabs start out by being little."

"That is correct," I said. "But why do you want the sheep to eat the little baobabs?"

He answered me at once, "Oh, come, come!" as if to say something that was clear.

And I had to make a great mental effort to solve this problem, without any assistance. As I learned, there were on the planet where the little prince lived, good plants and bad plants, like on all planets. So, there were good seeds from good plants and bad seeds from bad plants. But seeds are invisible. They sleep deep in the heart of the earth's darkness until a seed among them has the desire to wake up. Then this little seed will begin to stretch itself and begin to shyly push a charming small branch upward the sun harmlessly. If it is a small vegetable or flower, it should be let to grow. But when it is a bad plant, one must destroy it as soon as possible, the very first time that one notices it.

Now there were some bad seeds on the planet that was the home of the little prince. And these were the seeds of the baobab. The ground of that planet was filled with them. A baobab is something you will never, ever be able to remove if you take care of it too late. It spreads over the whole planet. It drills clear through it with its roots. And if the planet is too small, and the baobabs are too many, they split it into pieces...

"It is a question of daily habit," the little prince said to me later on. "When you've finished your own daily routine in the morning, then it is time to work on the daily routine of your planet with the greatest care. You must see to it that you pull up regularly all the baobabs, at the very first moment when they can be separated from the rosebushes which they looked so much like in their earliest youth. It is very boring work," the little prince added, "but it's very easy."

And one day he said to me: "You ought to make a beautiful drawing so your planet children can see exactly how all of this is. That would be very useful to them if they were to travel someday. Sometimes, there is no harm in putting off a piece of work until another day, but when it is a problem of baobabs, that always means disaster. I knew a planet where a lazy man lived. He ignored three little bushes ..."

The little prince described it to me. And I have made a drawing of that planet. I don't like to talk like a moral person, but the danger of the baobabs is not well known and it is dangerous for anyone who gets lost on a small planet. So I am breaking my character for the first time.
"Children," I say plainly, "watch out for the baobabs!"

My friends have been ignoring this danger for a long time without ever knowing it. That's why I have worked so hard on this drawing. The lesson that I show in the drawing

is worth the effort.

Perhaps you will ask me, "Why are there no other drawings in this book as amazing and powerful as this drawing of the baobabs?" The reply is simple. I have tried, but I have not been successful with the others. When I made the drawing of the baobabs, I was carried by a strong force of necessity.

Chapter 6

Oh, little prince! Bit by bit, I came to understand the secrets of your sad little life... For a long time, you had found your only enjoyment in the quiet joy of looking at the sunset.

I learned that new detail on the morning of the fourth day when you said to me:
"I really love sunsets. Come, let's go look at a sunset now."
"But we must wait," I said.
"Wait? For what?"
"For the sunset. We must wait until it is time."
At first, you seemed to be very surprised. And then you laughed to yourself. You said to me:
"I am always thinking that I am at home!"

It's true. Everyone knows that when it's noon in the United States, it's sunset in France. If you could fly to France in one minute, you could go straight into the sunset. Unfortunately, France is too far away. But on your tiny planet, all you need to do is move your chair a few steps forward. You can see the day end and the sun setting whenever you like...

"One day," you said to me, "I saw the sunset forty-four times!" And a little later you said: "You know I love the sunset when I am so sad..."
"Were you so sad on the day of the forty-four sunsets?" I asked.
But the little prince made no reply.

Chapter 7

On the fifth day, the secret of the little prince's life was uncovered for me. As always, it was because of the sheep. Suddenly, without any reason, and as if the question had been born of deep and silent thinking on his problem, he asked:

"A sheep—if it eats little bushes, does it eat flowers too?"

"A sheep eats anything it finds in its reach," I answered.

"Even flowers that have thorns?"

"Yes, even flowers that have thorns."

"Then the thorns—what use are they?"

I did not know. At that moment, I was very busy trying to unscrew a bolt in my engine. I was very much worried, for it was becoming to me that the breakdown of my plane was very serious. And I had so little drinking water left that I feared for the worst.

"The thorns—what use are they?" The little prince never let go of a question once he had asked it. As for me, I was upset over that bolt. And I answered with the first thing that came into my head:

"The thorns are of no use at all. Flowers have thorns because they are not kind!"

"Oh!" There was a moment of silence. Then the little prince suddenly answered with anger:

"I don't believe you! Flowers are weak creatures. They are innocent. They protect themselves as best they can. They believe that their thorns are terrible weapons..."

I did not answer. At that moment, I was saying to myself:

"If this bolt still won't turn, I am going to remove it with the hammer."

Again, the little prince stopped my thoughts:

"And you actually believe that the flowers-"

"Oh, no!" I cried. "No, no, no! I don't believe anything. I answered you with the first thing that came into my head. Don't you see—I am very busy with matters of consequence!"

He stared at me, thunderstruck. "Matters of consequence!" I had my hammer in my hand, my fingers black with engine-oil, bending down over this ugly object.

"You talk just like the grown-ups!"

That made me a little ashamed. But he went on with no mercy:

"You mix everything up together... You confuse everything..." He was really very angry. He tossed his golden, curly hair all over.

"I know a planet where there is one red-faced gentleman. He has never smelled a flower. He has never looked at a star. He has never loved anyone. He has never done anything in his life. He only adds up numbers. And all day he says over and over, just like you: 'I am busy with matters of consequence!' And that makes him increase with pride. But he is not a man. He is a mushroom!"

"A what?"

"A mushroom!" The little prince was now pale with anger.

"The flowers have been growing thorns for millions of years. For millions of years, the sheep have been eating them just the same. And is it not a matter of consequence to try to understand why the flowers work hard to make useless thorns? Is the war between the sheep and the flowers not important? Is this not more important than a fat red-faced gentleman's sums?"

"And if I know one flower who is unique in the world, who grows only on my planet, but one little sheep can destroy it in a single bite some morning, without any noise... Oh! You think that is not important!"

His face turned from white to red as he continued:

"If someone loves a flower, who grows only on one star, that is enough to make him happy to look at the stars. He can say to himself, 'Somewhere, my flower is there...' But if the sheep eats the flower, in one moment all his stars will be darkened... And you think that is not important!"

He could not say anything more. His words were choked

by crying. The night had fallen. I dropped my tools from my hands. Right now, my tools, thirst, or death did not matter. On one star, one planet, my planet, the Earth, there was a little prince who needed to be comforted.

I took him in my arms and rocked him. I said to him:

"The flower that you love is not in danger. I will draw you a mask for your sheep. I will draw you a fence to put around your flower. I will—" I did not know what to say to him. I felt uncomfortable and nervous. I did not know how I could reach him or where I could overtake him and go on hand in hand with him once more. The land of tears is such a secret place.

Chapter 8

Soon I learned to know this flower better. On the little prince's planet, the flowers had always been very simple. They had only one ring of petals. They took up no space at all. They did not cause trouble. One morning they would appear in the grass, and by night they would have faded peacefully away.

One day, a seed blew from somewhere. A new flower had come up and the little prince watched very closely over this small sprout. It was not like any other small sprouts on his planet. It might have been a new kind of baobab.

The shrub soon stopped growing and began to get ready to flower. The little prince saw the first sprouting of a huge bud. He felt at once that some kind of awesome thing must come up from it, but the flower was not satisfied to complete the plans for her beauty in the shelter of her green room.

She chose her colors with the greatest care. She dressed slowly. She set her petals one by one. She did not wish to go out into the world all messy, like the field flowers. It was only in the full brightness of her beauty that she wished to appear. Oh, yes! She was an attractive creature! And her fantastic beautify lasted for days and days.

Then one morning she suddenly showed herself. And after working with all this extremely careful detail, she yawned and said:

"Ah! I am hardly awake. Please excuse me. My petals are still all messy..."

But the little prince could not hold in his surprise:

"Oh! How beautiful you are!"

"Am I not?" the flower replied, sweetly. "And I was born at the same moment as the sun..."

The little prince could guess easily enough that she was too proud—but how exciting—she was!

"I think it is time for breakfast," she added a second later. "If you would kindly think about my needs—"

And the little prince, completely confused, went to look for fresh water. So, he took care of the flower. So, she began very quickly to stress him with her selfishness too. Honestly, it was difficult to deal with.

For example, one day, as she was speaking of her four thorns, she said to the little prince:

"Let the tigers come with their claws!"

"There are no tigers on my planet," the little prince disagreed.

"And tigers do not eat wild plants."

"I am not a wild plant," the flower replied, sweetly.

"Please excuse me ..."

"I am not at all afraid of tigers," she went on, "but I have a fear of wind. I guess you might have a screen for me?"

"A fear of wind—that is bad luck, for a plant," commented the little prince, and he added to himself, "This flower is a very complex creature..."

"At night I want you to put me under a glass cup. It is very cold where you live. In the place where I came from..." But she stopped talking to herself at that point. She had come from a seed. She could not have known anything of any other worlds. Embarrassed about being caught saying a lie, she coughed two or three times and tried to blame the little prince.

"The screen?"

"I was just going to look for it when you spoke to me..."

Then she forced herself to cough a little more so that he would suffer from regret. So the little prince, in spite of all the goodwill that came from his love, had soon started to doubt her. He had taken seriously words which were without importance. Finally, it made him very unhappy.

"I ought not to have

listened to her," he shared his thoughts with me one day. "No one ought to listen to the flowers. One should simply look at them and breathe their smell. My flower perfumed my whole planet, but I did not know how to enjoy all her grace. This story of claws, which upset me so much, should only have filled my heart with kindness and pity."

And he continued to share his thoughts:

"The fact is that I did not know how to understand anything! I should have judged by actions and not by words. She tossed her smell and her brightness over me. I should never

have run away from her... I should have noticed all the love that was behind her poor and little bad words. Flowers are so illogical! But I was too young to know how to love her..."

Chapter 9

I believe that for his escape, he used the movements of a group of wild birds. On the morning of his departure, he cleaned his planet perfectly. He carefully cleaned out his active volcanoes. He had two active volcanoes, and they were very helpful for heating his breakfast in the morning.

He also had one volcano that was dead. But, as he said, "One never knows!" So he cleaned out the dead volcano, too. If they are well cleaned, volcanoes burn slowly and steadily, without any explosions. Volcanic lava is like a fire in a fireplace. On our earth, we are surely much too small to clean out our volcanoes. That is why they bring so much trouble on us.

The little prince also pulled up the last little shoots of the baobabs with a certain sense of sadness. He believed that he would never want to return. However, on this last morning, all these familiar tasks seemed very precious to him. And when he watered the flower for the last time and prepared to place her under the shelter of her glass cup, he realized that he was very close to tears.

"Goodbye," he said to the flower.
But she made no answer.

"Goodbye," he said again. The flower coughed. But it was not because she had a cold. "I have been silly," she said to him at last. "I ask your forgiveness. Try to be happy..."

He was surprised by her lack of complaints. He stood there confused, the glass cup held in mid-air. He did not understand this quiet sweetness.

"Of course I love you," the flower said to him. "It is my fault that you have not known it all the time. That is not important. But you—you have been just as foolish as I have been. Try to be happy... Let the glass cup be. I don't need it anymore."

"But the wind..."

"My cold is not so bad as all that... The cool night air will do me good. I am a flower."

"But the animals..."

"Well, I must endure two or three worms if I wish to become friends with the butterflies. It seems that they are very beautiful. And if not the butterflies and the worms, who will call upon me? You will be far away..."

"As for the large animals, I am not at all afraid of any of them. I have my claws." And, she showed her four thorns. Then she added:

"Don't stay like this. You have decided to go away. Now go!" For she did not want him to see her crying. She was such a proud flower...

Chapter 10

He found himself in the neighborhood of the small planets 325, 326, 327, 328, 329, and 330. He began visiting them to add to his knowledge.

On the first of them, there lived a king. He wore a royal robe and white fur. He was seated on a chair which was simple and royal. "Ah! Here is a subject," cried the king when he saw the little prince coming.

And the little prince asked himself:

"How could he know me when he had never seen me before?" He did not know how the world is simplified for kings. To them, all men are subjects.

"Come closer, so that I may see you better," said the king, who felt proud of being a king over somebody at last.

The little prince looked everywhere to find a place to sit down, but all of the planet was filled and blocked by the king's amazing white fur clothes. So he remained standing upright.

And, since he was tired, he yawned.

"It is opposing to good manners to yawn in the presence of a king," the king said to him. "I forbid you to yawn."

"I can't help it. I can't stop myself," replied the little prince, totally ashamed. "I have come on a long journey, and I have had no sleep..."

"Ah, then," the king said. "I order you to yawn. It is years since I have seen anyone yawning. Yawns are objects of interest for me. Come now! Yawn again! It is an order."

"That scares me... I cannot any more..." the little prince said in a low voice, now completely abashed.

"Hum! Hum!" replied the king. "Then I—I order you sometimes to yawn and sometimes to—" He repeated words a little and seemed angry. What the king basically wanted was his authority to be respected. He didn't accept disobedience. He was an absolute king.

But because the king was a very good man, he made his orders reasonable. He would say, by way of example, "if I ordered a general to change himself into a sea bird, and if the general did not obey me, that would not be the fault of the general. It would be my fault."

"May I sit down?" There came a shy question from the little prince.

"I order you to do so," the king answered him, and he royally gathered in a fold of his fur cloak.

But the little prince was wondering... The planet was tiny. Over what could this king really rule?

"Sire," he said to him, "Would you excuse my asking you a question—"

"I order you to ask me a question," the king hurried to assure him.

"Sire, over what do you rule?"

"Over everything," said the king, with simplicity.

"Over everything?"

The king waved his hand towards the other planets and all the stars.

"Over all that?" asked the little prince.

"Over all that," the king answered.

For his rule was not only absolute: it was also universal.

"And the stars obey you?"

"Certainly they do," the king said. "They obey instantly. I do not allow disobedience."

This power was a thing for the little prince to wonder at. If he had been master of such force, he would have been able to watch the sunset, not forty-four times in one day, but seventy-two, or even a hundred, or even two hundred times, without ever having to move his chair.

And because he felt a bit sad as he remembered his little planet which he had left, he took up the courage to ask the king a favor: "I should like to see a sunset... Do me that kindness... Order the sun to set..."

"If I ordered a general to fly from one flower to another like a butterfly, or to write an awful drama, or to change himself into a sea bird, and if the general did not carry out the order, which one of us would be in the wrong?" the king asked. "The general, or myself?"

"You," said the little prince firmly.

"Exactly, one should require each person to do what each person can perform," the king went on. "First of all, accepted authority rests on reason. If you ordered your people to go and throw themselves into the sea, they would rise up in revolution. I have the right to require obedience because my orders are reasonable."

"Then my sunset?" the little prince reminded him: he never forgot a question once he had asked it.

"You shall have your sunset. I shall command it. But, according to my scientist, I shall wait until conditions are agreeable."

"When will that be?" questioned the little prince.

"Hum! Hum!" replied the king, and before saying anything else, he consulted a heavy yearbook. "Hum! Hum! That will be this evening... that will be at twenty minutes to eight. And you will see how well I am obeyed!"

The little prince yawned. He was feeling sorry about his lost sunset. And he was already beginning to be a little bored too. "I have nothing more to do here," he said to the king. "So I shall set out on my way again."

"Do not go," said the king, who was very proud of having a subject. "Do not go. I will make you a Minister!"

"Minister of what?"

"Minister of... of Justice!"

"But there is nobody here to judge!"

"We do not know that," the king said to him. "I have not yet made a complete tour of my kingdom. I am very old. There is no room for a cart and I'm tired of walking."

"Oh, but I have looked already!" said the little prince, turning around to check the other side of the planet once more. On that side, there was nobody at all...

"Then you shall judge yourself," the king answered, "that is the most difficult thing of all. It is much more difficult to judge oneself than to judge others. If you succeed in judging yourself rightly, then you are indeed a man of true wisdom."

"Yes," said the little prince, "but I can judge myself anywhere. I do not need to live on this planet."

"Hum! Hum!" said the king.

"I believe that somewhere on my planet, there is an old rat. I hear him at night. You can judge this old rat. Sometimes, you can judge him to death. Thus, his life will depend on your justice. But you will pardon him each time; for he must be treated with care. He is the only one we have."

"I do not like to judge anyone to death," replied the little prince, "And now I think I will go on my way."

"No," said the king.

But the little prince, having now completed his preparations for departure, had no wish to feel sorry for the old king.

"If you wish to be immediately obeyed," he said, "you should be able to give me a reasonable order. For example, you should order me to be gone by the end of one minute. It seems to me that conditions are agreeable..."

The king made no answer, so the little prince hesitated a moment. Then he took his leave with a sigh.

"I make you my Ambassador," the king called out, quickly. He had an awesome mood of authority.

"The grown-ups are very strange," the little prince said to himself as he continued on his journey.

Chapter 11

The second planet was settled by a proud man. "Ah! Ah! I am about to receive a visit from an admirer!" he cried out from far away when he first saw the little prince coming. For proud men, all other men are admirers.

"Good morning," said the little prince. "That is an odd hat you are wearing."

"It is a hat for greetings," the proud man replied. "It is to raise in greeting when people praise me. Unfortunately, nobody passes this way."

"Yes?" said the little prince, who did not understand what the proud man was talking about.

"Clap your hands, one against the other," the proud man directed him. The little prince clapped his hands. The proud man raised his hat in a modest greeting.

"This is more entertaining than the visit to the king," the little prince said to himself.

And he began again to clap his hands, one against the other. The proud man again raised his hat in greeting. After five minutes of this exercise, the little prince grew tired of the game's repetition.

"And what should one do to make the hat come down?" he asked.

But the proud man did not hear him. Proud people never hear anything but praise.

"Do you really admire me very much?" he demanded of the little prince.

"What does that mean—'admire'?"

"To admire means that you consider me as the most handsome, the best-dressed, the richest, and the most intelligent man on this planet."

"But you are the only man on your planet!"

"Do me this kindness. Admire me just the same."

"I admire you," said the little prince, moving his shoulders lightly, "but what about that would interest you so much?" And the little prince went away. "The grown-ups are certainly very odd," he said to himself, as he continued on his journey.

Chapter 12

The next planet was occupied by an alcoholic. This was a very short visit, but it made the little prince drop into a deep depression.

"What are you doing there?" he said to the alcoholic, whom he found settled down before a collection of empty bottles and also a collection of full bottles.

"I am drinking," replied the alcoholic, with a gloomy mood.

"Why are you drinking?" demanded the little prince.

"So that I may forget," replied the alcoholic.

"Forget what?" questions the little prince, who already was sorry for him.

"Forget that I am ashamed," the alcoholic confessed, dropping his head.

"Ashamed of what?" repeated the little prince, who wanted to help him.

"Ashamed of drinking!" The alcoholic brought his speech to an end and shut himself up in an unshakable silence.

And the little prince went away, confused. "The grown-ups are certainly very, very odd," he said to himself, as he continued on his journey.

Chapter 13

The fourth planet belonged to a businessman. This man was so much occupied that he did not even raise his head at the little prince's arrival. "Good morning," the little prince said to him. "Your cigarette has gone out."

"Three and two make five. Five and seven make twelve. Twelve and three make fifteen. Good morning. Fifteen and seven make twenty-two. Twenty-two and six make twenty-eight. I haven't time to light it again. Twenty-six and five make thirty-one. Phew! Then that makes five-hundred-and-one-million, six-hundred-twenty-two-thousand, seven-hundred-thirty-one (501,622,731)."

"Five hundred million what?" asked the little prince.

"Eh? Are you still there? Five-hundred-and-one million... I can't stop... I have so much to do! I am concerned with important work. I don't amuse myself with nonsense. Two and five make seven."

"Five-hundred-and-one million what?" repeated the little prince, who never let go of a question once he had asked it. The businessman raised his head.

"During the fifty-four years that I have lived on this planet, I have been disturbed only three times. The first time was twenty-two years ago when some dizzy goose fell from Goodness knows where. He made an awful noise that echoed all over the place and I made four mistakes in my addition.

"The second time, eleven years ago, I was disturbed by an attack of joint pain. I don't get enough exercise. I have no time to laze around. The third time—well, this is it! As I was saying, five-hundred-and-one millions—"

"Millions of what?" The businessman suddenly realized that there was no chance of peace until he answered this question.

"Millions of those little objects," he said, "which one sometimes sees in the sky."

"Flies?"

"Oh, no. Little shining objects."

"Bees?"

"Oh, no. Little golden objects that set lazy men to unrealistic dreaming. As for me, I am concerned with important work. There is no time for unrealistic dreaming in my life."

"Ah! You mean the stars?"

"Yes, that's it. The stars."

"And what do you do with five-hundred millions of stars?"

"Five-hundred-and-one million, six-hundred-twenty-two thousand, seven-hundred-thirty-one. I am concerned with important work. I am an exact person."

"And what do you do with these stars?"

"What do I do with them?"

"Yes."

"Nothing. I own them."

"You own the stars?"

"Yes."

"But I have already seen a king who—"

"Kings do not own; they rule over. It is a very different matter."

"And what good does it do you to own the stars?"

"It does me the good of making me rich."

"And what good does it do you to be rich?"

"It makes it possible for me to buy more stars if any are discovered."

"This man," the little prince said to himself, "reasons a little like my poor alcoholic..." Nevertheless, he still had some more questions.

"How is it possible for one to own the stars?"

"To whom do they belong?" the businessman replied angrily.

"I don't know. To nobody."

"Then they belong to me because I was the first person to think of it."

"Is that all that is necessary?"

"Certainly. When you find a diamond that belongs to nobody, it is yours. When you discover an island that belongs to nobody, it is yours. When you get an idea before anyone else, you put a copyright on it: it is yours. Just like that: I own the stars because nobody else before me ever thought of

owning them."

"Yes, that is true," said the little prince. "And what do you do with them?"

"I manage them," replied the businessman. "I count them and recount them. It is difficult, but I am a man who is naturally interested in important work."

The little prince was still not satisfied. "If I owned a silk scarf," he said, "I could put it around my neck and take it away with me. If I owned a flower, I could pick that flower and take it away with me. But you cannot pick the stars from heaven..."

"No. But I can put them in the bank."

"Whatever does that mean?"

"That means that I write the number of my stars on a

little paper and then I put this paper in a drawer and lock it with a key."

"And that is all?"

"That is enough," said the businessman.

"It is entertaining," thought the little prince. "It is rather poetic, but it is of no great importance." On matters of importance, the little prince had ideas which were very different from those of the grownups.

"I myself own a flower," he continued his conversation with the businessman, "which I water every day. I own three volcanoes, which I clean out every week. It is useful to my volcanoes, and it is useful to my flower, that I own them."

"But you are of no use to the stars..." The businessman opened his mouth, but he found nothing to say in answer. The little prince went away. "The grown-ups are certainly altogether very unusual," he said simply, talking to himself as he continued on his journey.

Chapter 14

The fifth planet was very strange. It was the smallest of all. There was just enough room on it for a street lamp and a lamplighter. The little prince could not understand the reason for the use of a street lamp and a lamplighter on a planet which had no people and not one house.

But he said to himself, "It may be that this man is unreasonable, but he is not so unreasonable as the king, the proud man, the businessman, and the alcoholic. At least his work has some meaning."

"When he lights his street lamp, it looks like he brought one more star to life or one flower. When he puts out his lamp, he sends the flower or the star to sleep. That is a beautiful job. And since it is beautiful, it is truly useful."

When he arrived on the planet, he respectfully greeted the lamplighter. "Good morning. Why have you just put out your lamp?"

"Those are the orders," replied the lamplighter. "Good morning."

"What are the orders?"

"The orders are that I put out my lamp. Good evening." And he lighted his lamp again.

"But why have you just lighted it again?"

"Those are the orders," replied the lamplighter.

"I do not understand," said the little prince.

"There is nothing to understand," said the lamplighter. "Orders are orders. Good morning." And he put out his lamp, then he wiped his forehead with a handkerchief with red squares.

"I follow a terrible line of work. In the old days, it was reasonable. I put the lamp out in the morning, and in the evening, I lighted it again. I had the rest of the day for leisure and the rest of the night for sleep."

"And the orders have been changed since that time?"

"The orders have not been changed," said the lamplighter. "That is the disaster! From year to year, the planet has turned more rapidly, and the orders have not been changed!"

"Then what?" asked the little prince.

"Then the planet now makes a complete turn every minute, and I no longer have a single second for rest. Once every minute I have to light my lamp and put it out!"

"That is very funny! A day lasts only one minute on this planet!"

"It is not funny at all!" said the lamplighter. "While we have been talking together, a month has gone by."

"A month?"

"Yes, a month. Thirty minutes. Thirty days. Good evening." And he lighted his lamp again.

As the little prince watched him, he felt that he loved this lamplighter who was so faithful to his orders. Then he remembered how he moved his chair back to seek the sunsets, and he wanted to help his friend.

I follow a terrible profession.

"You know," he said, "I can tell you a way you can rest whenever you want to..."

"I always want to rest," said the lamplighter. It is possible for a man to be faithful and lazy at the same time.

The little prince went on with his explanation: "Your planet is so small that three steps will take you all the way around it. When you want to rest, you can walk slowly and the day will last as long as you like."

"That doesn't do me much good," said the lamplighter. "The one thing I love to do is to sleep."

"Then you're unlucky," said the little prince.

"I am unlucky," said the lamplighter. "Good morning." And he put out his lamp.

The little prince said to himself, as he continued on his journey, "That man would be hated by all the others: by the king, by the proud man, by the alcoholic, and by the businessman. Nevertheless, he is the only one of them who does not look ridiculous. Perhaps that is because he is thinking of something outside of himself."

He breathed a sigh of regret, and said to himself, again: "That man is the only one of them who I could have made my friend, but his planet is really too small. There is no room on it for two people..." What the little prince hid in his heart was that he was sorry most of all to leave this planet because it was blessed every day with 1,440 sunsets!

Chapter 15

The sixth planet was ten times larger than the last one. An old gentleman who wrote large books lived there. "Oh, look! Here is an explorer!" he shouted to himself when he saw the little prince coming.

The little prince sat down on the table and breathed quickly. He had already traveled so much and so far!

"Where do you come from?" the old gentleman said to him.

"What is that big book?" said the little prince. "What are you doing?"

"I am a geographer," said the old gentleman.

"What is a geographer?" asked the little prince.

"A geographer is a scholar who knows the location of all the seas, rivers, towns, mountains, and deserts."

"That is very interesting," said the little prince.

"At last, here is a man who has a real job!" And he looked around him at the planet of the geographer. It was the most amazing and grand that he had ever seen.

"Your planet is very beautiful," he said. "Has it any oceans?"

"I couldn't tell you," said the geographer.

"Ah!" The little prince was disappointed. "Has it any mountains?"

"I couldn't tell you," said the geographer.

"And towns, and rivers, and deserts?"

"I couldn't tell you that, either."

"But you are a geographer!"

"Exactly," the geographer said. "But I am not an explorer. I haven't a single explorer on my planet. It is not the geographer who goes out to count the towns, the rivers, the mountains, the seas, the oceans, and the deserts. The geographer is much too important to waste time. He does not leave his desk."

The scientist went on, "So he receives the explorers in his study. He asks them questions and he writes down the memories of their travels. And if the memories of the explorers seem interesting to him, the geographer orders an investgation into that explorer's moral character."

"Why is that?"

"Because an explorer who told lies would bring disaster on the books of the geographer, so would an explorer who drank too much."

"Why is that?" asked the little prince.

"Because drunken men see double. Then the geographer would note two mountains when there was only one."

"I know someone," said the little prince, "who would make a bad explorer."

"That is possible."

"Then, when the moral character of the explorer is shown

to be good, a search is ordered about the discovery."

"One goes to see it?"

"No. That would be too complicated. But one requires the explorer to supply data. For example, if the discovery in question is that of a large mountain, one requires that large stones be brought back from it."

The geographer was suddenly moved to joy. "But you—you come from far away! You are an explorer! You shall describe your planet to me!" And, having opened his big book, the geographer sharpened his pencil. The reports of explorers are written down first in pencil. One waits until the explorer has supplied data before writing them down in ink.

"Well?" said the geographer hopefully.

"Oh, where I live," said the little prince, "it is not very interesting. It is all so small. I have three volcanoes. Two volcanoes are active, and the other one is dead. But one never knows."

"One never knows," said the geographer.

"I also have a flower."

"We do not record flowers," said the geographer.

"Why is that? The flower is the most beautiful thing on my planet!"

"We do not record them," said the geographer, "because they are short life span."

"What does that mean, 'short life span'?"

"Geography books are concerned with matters of importance." said the scientist. "They never become old-fashioned. It is very rarely that a mountain changes its position. It is very rarely that an ocean empties of its waters. We write of unchanging things."

"But dead volcanoes may come to life again," the little prince interrupted. "What does that mean— 'short life span'?"

"Whether volcanoes are dead or alive, it comes to the same thing for us," said the geographer. "The thing that matters to us is the mountain. It does not change."

"But what does that mean— 'short life span'?" repeated the little prince, who never in his life had let go of a question.

"It means, 'that which is in danger of speedy disappearance.'"

"Is my flower in danger of speedy disappearance?"

"Certainly, it is."

"My flower is short life span," the little prince said to himself, "and she has only four thorns to defend herself against the world. And I have left her on my planet, all alone!" That was his first moment of regret.

But he took courage once more. "What place would you advise me to visit now?" he asked.

"The planet Earth," replied the geographer. "It is well known."

And the little prince went away, thinking of his flower.

Chapter 16

So then the seventh planet was the Earth. The Earth is not just a normal planet! There are 111 kings (not forgetting the African kings among them), 7,000 geographers, 900,000 businessmen, 7,500,000 alcoholics, 311,000,000 proud men-that is to say- about 2,000,000,000 grown-ups.

To give you an idea of the size of the Earth, I will tell you that before electricity, it was necessary to have 462,511 lamplighters. Over the whole of the six continents, 462,511 lamplighters were needed.

Seen from a slight distance, that would make an excellent show. The movements of this army would be controlled like those of the ballet dancers in the opera.

First, the lamplighters of New Zealand and Australia would come. Having set the light of their lamps, these people would go off to sleep. Next, the lamplighters of China and Siberia would enter for their steps in the dance, and then they too would go backstage.

After that, the lamplighters of Russia and the Indies would come; then those of Africa and Europe; then those of South America would come; and then those of North America.

And never would they make a mistake in the order of their entry on the stage. It was amazing. Only the man who was in charge of the single lamp at the North Pole and his friend who was responsible for the single lamp at the South Pole—only these two would live freely. They would be busy twice a year.

Chapter 17

When one wishes to play the wit, he sometimes walks away a little from the truth. I have not been fully honest in what I have told you about the lamplighters. And I realize that I gave a false idea of our planet to those who do not know it.

Men occupy a very small place on Earth. If the two billion people on its surface were all to stand upright, they could easily be put into one public square thirty-two kilometers long and thirty-two kilometers wide. If they were crowded together, as they sometimes do for big public gatherings, all humanity

When the little prince arrived on the Earth, he was very much surprised not to see any people.

could be piled up on a small Pacific island.

The grown-ups will not believe you when you tell them that. They imagine that they fill a great deal of space. They wish they could be as important as the baobabs. You should advise them to make their own calculations. They love figures, and that will please them. Do not waste your time on this extra task. It is unnecessary. You have trust in me.

When the little prince arrived on the Earth, he was very much surprised not to see any people. He was beginning to be afraid that he had come to the wrong planet. At that time, a coil of gold flashed across the sand.

"Good evening," said the little prince gently.

"Good evening," said the snake.

"What planet is this on which I have come down?" asked the little prince.

"This is the Earth; this is Africa," the snake answered.

"Ah! Then there are no people on the Earth?"

"This is the desert. There are no people in the desert. The Earth is large," said the snake.

The little prince sat down on a stone and raised his eyes toward the sky. "I wonder if the stars are alight in heaven so that one day, each one of us may find his own star again..." he said. "Look at my planet. It is right there above us. But how far away it is!"

"It is beautiful," the snake said. "What has brought you here?"

"I have been having some trouble with a flower," said the little prince.

"Ah!" said the snake. And they were both silent.

"Where are the men?" the little prince, at last, started the conversation again. "It is a little lonely in the desert..."

"It is also lonely among men," the snake said.

The little prince stared at him for a long time. "You are a funny animal," he said at last. "You are no thicker than a finger..."

"But I am more powerful than the finger of a king," said the snake.

The little prince smiled. "You are not very powerful. You haven't even any feet. You cannot even travel..."

"I can carry you farther than any ship could take you," said the snake. He twisted himself around the little prince's ankle, like a golden chain. "Whomever I touch, I send back to the earth from where he came," the snake spoke again.

"But you are pure and true, and you come from a star... You move me to pity—you are so weak on this Earth made of stone," the snake said. "I can help you, someday, if you grow too homesick for your own planet. I can-"

"Oh! I understand you very well," said the little prince. "But why do you always speak in riddles?"

"I solve them all," said the snake. And they were both silent.

Chapter 18

The little prince crossed the desert and met with only one flower. It was a flower with three petals— a flower of no importance at all.

"Good morning," said the little prince.

"Good morning," said the flower.

"Where are the men?" the little prince asked gently.

The flower had once seen people passing. "Men?" she echoed. "I think there are six or seven of them alive. I saw them several years ago, but one never knows where to find them. The wind blows them away. They have no roots, and that makes their life very difficult."

"Goodbye," said the little prince.

"Goodbye," said the flower.

Chapter 19

After that, the little prince climbed a high mountain. The only mountains he had ever known were the three volcanoes, which came up to his knees. And he used the dead volcano as a chair. "From a mountain as high as this one," he said to himself, "I shall be able to see the whole planet at once, and all the people..." But he saw nothing but peaks of rock that were sharpened like needles.

"Good morning," he said gently.

"Good morning, Good morning, Good morning," answered the echo.

"Who are you?" said the little prince.

"Who are you, Who are you, Who are you?" answered the echo.

"Be my friend. I am all alone," he said.

"I am all alone, all alone, all alone," answered the echo.

"What an odd planet!" he thought. "It is completely dry and pointed and tough and grim. And the people have no imagination. They repeat whatever anyone says to them... On my planet I had a flower; she was always the first to speak..."

Chapter 20

But it happened that after walking for a long time through sand and rocks, that at last, the little prince came upon a road. And all roads lead to the houses of men.

"Good morning," he said. He was standing before the rose garden.
"Good morning," said the roses.
The little prince looked at them. They all looked like his flower.

"Who are you?" he demanded. He was shocked.
"We are roses," the roses said. And he was overcome with sadness. His flower had told him that she was the only one of her kind in all the universe and here were five thousand of them in one single garden!

"She would be very much annoyed," he said to himself, "if she should see that, she would cough most severely, and she would pretend that she was dying. And I would be forced to pretend that I was nursing her back to life. If I did not do that, to teach me a lesson, she would really allow herself to die..."

Then he went on with his thoughts: "I thought that I was rich, with a flower that was unique in all the world, but all I had was a common rose. A common rose, and three volcanoes that come up to my knees— and one of them is perhaps dead forever... That doesn't make me a very great prince..." And he lay down in the grass and cried.

Chapter 21

It was then that the fox appeared. "Good morning," said the fox.

"Good morning," the little prince responded politely, although when he turned around, he saw nothing.

"I am right here," the voice said, "under the apple tree."

"Who are you?" asked the little prince, and he added, "You are very pretty to look at."

"I am a fox," the fox said.

"Come and play with me," proposed the little prince. "I am so unhappy."

"I cannot play with you," the fox said. "I am not tamed."

"Ah! Sorry," said the little prince. But, after some thought, he added:

"What does that mean—'tame'?"

"You do not live here," said the fox. "What are looking for?"

"I am looking for men," said the little prince. "What does that mean —'tame'?"

"Men," said the fox. "They have guns, and they hunt. It is very concerning. They also raise chickens. These are their only interests.

"Are you looking for chickens?"

"No," said the little prince. "I am looking for friends. What does that mean, 'tame'?"

"It is an act too often ignored," said the fox. It means to build up ties."

"To build up ties'?"

"Just that." said the fox.

"To me, you are still nothing more than a little boy who is just like a hundred thousand other little boys. And I have no need of you. Also, you have no need of me. To you, I am nothing more than a fox like a hundred thousand other foxes. But if you tame me, then we shall need each other. To me, you will be unique in all the world. To you, I shall be unique in all the world..."

"I am beginning to understand," said the little prince. "There is a flower... I think that she has tamed me..."

"It is possible," said the fox. "On Earth, all kinds of things happen."

"Oh, but this is not on the Earth!" said the little prince.
The fox seemed confused and very interested. "On another planet?"

"Yes."

"Are there hunters on that planet?"

"No."

"Ah, that is interesting! Are there chickens?"

"No."

"Nothing is perfect," sighed the fox.

But he came back to his idea. "My life is unchanging," the fox said. "I hunt chickens; men hunt me. All the chickens are just alike and all the men are just alike. And now, I am a little bored."

"But if you tame me, it will be the sun came to shine on my life. I shall know the sound of a step that will be different from all the others. Other steps send me back under the ground. But your steps will call me out of my shelter."

"And then look: you see the grain fields over there? I do not eat bread. Wheat is no use to me. The wheat fields have nothing to say to me. And that is sad. But you have golden hair. Think about that when you tamed me! The golden grain will bring me back to the thought of you. And I shall love to listen to the wind in the wheat..."

The fox stared at the little prince for a long time. "Please— tame me!" the fox said.

"I want to, very much," the little prince replied. "But I don't have much time. I have friends to find, and a great many things to understand."

"Men only understand the things that they tame," said the fox. "Men have no more time to understand anything. They buy things all ready made at the shops. But there is no shop where one can buy friendship, and so men have no friends anymore. If you want a friend, tame me..."

"What must I do, to tame you?" asked the little prince.

"You must be very patient," replied the fox. "First, you will sit down at a little distance from me in the grass. I shall look at you out of the corner of my eye, and you will say nothing. Words are the source of misunderstandings. But you will sit a little closer to me, every day..."

The next day the little prince came back. "It would have been better to come back at the same hour," said the fox. "For example, if you come at four o'clock in the afternoon, then at three o'clock I shall begin to be happy. I shall feel happier and happier as the hour advances. But if you come at just any time, I shall never know at what hour my heart will be ready to greet you..."

"One must keep the right ceremony..."

"What is a ceremony?" asked the little prince.

"Those also are actions too often ignored," said the fox. "The ceremony is what make one day different from other days, and one hour from other hours.

"For example, there is a ceremony among my hunters. Every Thursday they dance with the village girls. So Thursday is a wonderful day for me! I can take a walk as far as the vineyards. But if the hunters danced at any time, every day would be like every other day, and I would never have any vacation at all."

So the little prince tamed the fox. And when the hour of his departure came closer-"Ah," said the fox, "I shall cry."

"It is your own fault," said the little prince. "I never wished you any sort of harm, but you wanted me to tame you..."

"Yes, that is so," said the fox.

"But now you are going to cry!" said the little prince.

"Yes, that is so," said the fox.

"Then it has done you no good at all!"

"It has done me good, because of the golden wheat fields," said the fox. And then he added, "Go and look again at the roses. You will understand now that your rose is unique in all the world. Then come back to say goodbye to me, and I will give you the present of a secret."

The little prince went away to look again at the roses. "You are not at all like my rose," he said. "No one has tamed you and you have tamed no one. You are like my fox when I first knew him. He was only a fox like a hundred thousand other foxes, but I have made him my friend, and now he is unique in all the world." And the roses were very much ashamed.

"You are beautiful, but you are empty," he went on. "No one could die for you. Ordinary people would think that my rose looked just like you. But she is more important than all the hundreds of you other roses, because it is she that I have watered, put under the glass cup, sheltered behind the screen, killed the worms for (except the two or three that we saved to become butterflies). And I have listened to her when she complained, said prideful things, or even when she said nothing, because she is my rose."

And he went back to meet the fox. "Goodbye," he said.

"Goodbye," said the fox. "And now here is my secret: It is only with the heart that one can see rightly. What is essential is invisible to the eye."

"What is essential is invisible to the eye," the little prince repeated so that he would be sure to remember.

"You have wasted time on your rose and that is what makes your rose so important."

"I have wasted time for my rose—" said the little prince, so that he would be sure to remember.

"Men have forgotten this truth," said the fox. "But you must not forget it. You become responsible for what you have tamed. You are responsible for your rose..."

"I am responsible for my rose," the little prince repeated so that he would be sure to remember.

Chapter 22

"Good morning," said the little prince.

"Good morning," said the railway switchman.

"What do you do here?" the little prince asked.

"I organize travelers, in groups of a thousand," said the switchman. "And I send off the trains with the groups: now to the right, now to the left."

And an express train full of light shook the switchman's cabin as it rushed by with a loud sound like thunder.

"They are in a great hurry," said the little prince. "What are they looking for?"

"Not even the railway driver knows that," said the switchman.

And a second express train full of light thundered by in the opposite direction.

"Are they coming back already?" demanded the little prince.

"These are not the same ones," said the switchman. "It is an exchange."

"Were they not satisfied where they were?" asked the little prince.

"No one is ever satisfied where he is," said the switchman.

And they heard the loud sound of thunder from a third fully lighted express train.

"Are they following the first travelers?" demanded the little prince.

"They are following nothing at all," said the switchman. "They are asleep in there, or, if they are not asleep, they are yawning. Only the children are flattening their noses against the windows."

"Only the children know what they are looking for," said the little prince. "They waste their time over a doll, and it becomes very important to them; and if anybody takes it away from them, they cry..."

"They are lucky," the switchman said.

Chapter 23

"Good morning," said the little prince.

"Good morning," said the merchant. This was a merchant who sold pills that take away feelings of thirst. You only need to take one pill a week and you will not be thirsty.

"Why are you selling those?" asked the little prince.

"Because they save a huge amount of time," said the merchant. "With these pills, you save fifty-three minutes every week. This result was calculated by experts."

"And what do I do with those fifty-three minutes?"

"Anything you like..."

"If I had fifty-three minutes to spend as I liked," said the little prince to himself, "I would walk towards a spring of fresh water."

Chapter 24

It was now the eighth day since I had had my accident in the desert. I had listened to the story of the merchant. I was drinking the last drop of my water.

"Ah," I said to the little prince, "these memories of yours are very sweet, but I have not yet repaired my plane. I have no more water to drink, and I would be very happy if I could walk toward a spring of fresh water!"

"My friend the fox-" the little prince said to me.
"My dear little man, this is not a matter that has anything to do with the fox!"
"Why not?"
"Because I am about to die of thirst..."
He did not follow my thoughts, and he answered me:
"It is a good thing to have had a friend, even if we are about to die. I am very glad to have had a fox as a friend..."

"He has no way of guessing the danger," I said to myself. "He has never been hungry or thirsty." But he looked at me steadily and replied to my thought:
"I am thirsty, too. Let us look for a well..."
I made a gesture of tiredness. It is strange to look for a well in a huge desert like this. Nevertheless, we started walking.

When we had walked slowly along for several hours, the

darkness fell, and the stars began to come out. Thirst had given me a fever, so I looked at the stars as if I were in a dream. The little prince's last words came back into my memory:

"Then you are thirsty, too?" I demanded. But he did not reply to my question. He only said to me:

"Water may also be good for the heart..."
I did not understand this answer, but I said nothing. I knew very well that it was impossible to ask him again.

He was tired. He sat down. I sat down beside him. And he spoke again:

"The stars are beautiful, because of a flower that cannot be seen."

I replied, "Yes, that is so." And I looked across the hills of sand without saying anything more. The hills of sand were laid out before us in the moonlight.

"The desert is beautiful," the little prince said.
And that was true. I have always loved the desert. While we sat down in the desert sand, we could see and hear nothing. But through the silence, something was moving and shining...

"What makes the desert beautiful," said the little prince, "is that somewhere it hides a well..."
I was surprised by a sudden understanding of that secret of the sands. The desert is beautiful because there is water one cannot see.

When I was a little boy, I lived in an old house, and legend told us there was a treasure inside. No one had ever known how to find it, but the legend cast a spell over that house. My home was hiding a secret in the depths of its heart...

"Yes," I said to the little prince. "The house, the stars, the desert-what gives them their beauty is something that is invisible!"

"I am glad," he said, "that you agree with my fox."

As the little prince dropped off to sleep, I took him in my arms and set out walking once more. I felt deeply touched. It seemed to me that I was carrying a very fragile treasure. It seemed to me that there was nothing more fragile on the Earth. In the moonlight, I looked at his forehead, his closed eyes, and his hair that moved in the wind. I said to myself:

"What I see here is nothing but a shell. What is most important is invisible..."

The little prince smiles. I say to myself, again:

"What touches my heart about this little prince who is sleeping here is his loyalty to a flower—I can see how he loves that flower..." And I felt him becoming more weak. I felt the need of protecting him as if he himself were like a fire that would blow out in the wind... And, as I continued walking, I found water in the morning.

Chapter 25

"Men," said the little prince, "set off on express trains, but they do not know what they are looking for. Then they rush about, and get excited, and turn around and around..." And he added: "It is not worth the trouble..."

The well that we found was not like the wells of the Sahara. The wells of the Sahara are just holes dug in the sand. This one was like a well in a village, but there was no village here. I thought I must be dreaming...

"It is strange," I said to the little prince. "Everything is ready for use: the well-wheel, the bucket, and the rope..." He laughed, touched the rope, and set the well-wheel to working. The well-wheel made a noise, like an old weather vane pointing the wind's direction.

"Do you hear?" said the little prince. "We have wakened the well, and it is singing..." I did not want him to tire himself with the rope.
"Leave this rope to me," I said. "It is too heavy for you."

I pulled the bucket slowly to the edge of the well and set it there. I felt tired, but I was happy because I did my job. The song of the well-wheel was still in my ears, and I could see the sunlight shining on the moving water.
"I am thirsty for this water," said the little prince. "Give me

some of it to drink..."

And I understood what he had been looking for. I raised the bucket to his lips. He drank with his eyes closed. It was as sweet as some special festival treat. This water was indeed different from ordinary water. Its sweetness was born of the walk under the stars, the song of the well-wheel, the effort of my arms. It was good for the heart, like a present. When I was a little boy, the lights of the Christmas tree, the music of church worship, and the kindness of smiling faces, used to be part of the happiness of the gifts I received.

"The men where you live raise five thousand roses in the garden," said the little prince. "But they do not find in it what they are looking for."

"They do not find it," I replied.

"Ah, but what they are looking for could be found in one single rose, or in a little water."

"Yes, that is true," I said.

And the little prince added: "But the eyes are blind. One must look with the heart..."

I drank the water. I breathed easily. At sunrise, the sand is the color of honey. And that honey color was making me happy, too. Then what brought me, this sense of heartbreak?

"You must keep your promise," said the little prince as he sat down beside me once more.

"What promise?"

"You know—a mask for my sheep... I am responsible for this flower..."

I took my rough drafts of drawings out of my pocket. The little prince looked them over and laughed as he said:
"Your baobabs—they look a little like cabbages."
"Oh, really? Hm..."
"Your fox—his ears look a little like horns, and they are too long." And he laughed again.
"You are not fair, little prince," I said. "I don't know how to draw anything except a boa snake from the outside and from the inside."
"Oh, that will be all right," he said, "children understand."

He laughed, touched the rope, and set the pulley to working.

So then I made a pencil sketch of a mask. And as I gave it to him, my heart was broken. "You have plans that I do not know about," I said. But he did not answer me. He said to me instead:
"You know—my fall to the earth...

Tomorrow will be its anniversary."

Then, after a silence, he went on: "I came down very near here." And he turned red. And once again, without understanding why, I had a strange sense of sorrow.

But one question came up to me:
"You were walking alone a thousand miles from any town... Then it was not by chance that in the morning when I first met you a week ago. Were you on your way back to the place where you landed?" The little prince turned red again.

And I added, with some delay:
"Perhaps it was because of the anniversary?" The little prince turned red once more. He never answered questions, but when his face changed; that meant "Yes."

"Ah," I said to him, "I am a little frightened—"

But he stopped me. "Now, you must work. You must return to your engine. I will be waiting for you here. Come back tomorrow evening..."

But I was uncomfortable. I remembered the fox. If you are tamed by someone, you could get teary-eyed...

Chapter 26

Beside the well, there was part of an old stone wall. When I came back from my work, the next evening, I saw my little prince from a little distance. He was sitting on top of a wall with his feet dropping over the edge.

And I heard him say:

"Then you don't remember. This is not the exact spot."

Another voice must have answered him, for he replied to it:

"Yes, yes! It is the right day, but this is not the place."

I continued my walk toward the wall. I did not see or hear anyone. But the little prince replied once again:

"—Exactly. You will see where my track begins, in the sand. You have nothing to do but wait for me there. I shall be there tonight."

I was only twenty meters from the wall and I still saw nothing. After a silence, the little prince spoke again:

"You have good poison? You are sure that it will not make me hurt for too long?"

I stopped in my tracks. My heart was broken to pieces, but I still did not understand.

"Now go away," said the little prince. "I want to get down from the wall."

I dropped my eyes to the foot of the wall—and I jumped

into the air. In front of me was a yellow snake that can end life in thirty seconds.

Even as I was getting my revolver, I stepped back fast, but when the snake heard the noise I made, he let himself move across the sand, and, in no hurry, disappeared, with a light sound between the stones.

I reached the wall just in time to catch my little man in my arms; his face was white as snow.

"What does this mean?" I demanded. "Why are you talking with snakes?" I had untied the golden scarf that he always wore. I had wetted the side of his forehead and given him some water to drink.

And now I did not dare ask him any more questions. He looked at me very seriously and put his arms around my neck. I felt his heart beating like the heart of a dying bird who was shot with someone's gun...

"I am glad that you found out what was wrong with your engine," he said. "Now you can go back home—"

"How do you know about that?" I was coming to tell him that my work was successful, better than I had expected. He made no answer to my question, but he added:

"I am also going back home today..."

Then, sadly— "It is much farther... It is much more difficult..."
I realized that an unexpected something was happening. I
was holding him close in my arms as if he were a little child.
And yet it seemed to me that he was rushing headlong
into a deep place where I could not stop him...

His look was very serious like someone lost far away.
"I have your sheep. And I have the sheep's box. And
I have the mask..." And he gave me a sad smile. I waited
for a long time. I could see that he was getting well little
by little.

"Dear little man," I said
to him, "you are afraid..."
He was afraid; there was
no doubt about that. But
he laughed lightly.

"I shall be much more
afraid this evening..."
Once again, I felt frozen by the sense of something destroyed.
And I knew that I could not hear that laugh anymore. For me,
it was like a spring of fresh water in the desert.

"Little man," I said, "I want to hear you laugh again." But
he said to me:
"Tonight, it will be a year... My star can be found right
above the place where I came to the Earth, a year ago..."

"Little man," I said, "tell me that it is only a bad dream—this event of the snake, and the meeting-place, and the star..." But he did not answer my plea. He said to me, instead:

"The thing that is important is the thing that is not seen..."

"Yes, I know..."

"It is just as it is with the flower. If you love a flower that lives on a star, it is sweet to look at the sky at night. All the stars are blooming with flowers..."

"Yes, I know..."

"It is just as it is with the water. Because of the well-wheel and the rope, what you gave me to drink was like music. You remember—how good it was."

"Yes, I know..."

"And at night you will look up at the stars. Where I live, everything is so small that I cannot show you where my star is to be found. But it is better, because my star will just be one of the stars for you. And so you will love to watch all the stars in the heavens... They will all be your friends. And, besides, I am going to make you a present..."

He laughed again.

"Ah, little prince, dear little prince! I love to hear that laugh!"

"That is my present. Just that. It will be as it was when we drank the water..."

"What are you trying to say?"

"All men have the stars," he answered, "but they are not the same stars for different people. For some who are travelers, the stars are guides. For others, they are no more than little lights in the sky. For scholars, they are problems. For my businessman, they were wealth."

"But all these stars are silent. You will have the stars as no one else has them-"
"What are you trying to say?"
"In one of the stars, I shall be living. In one of them, I shall be laughing. And so it will be as if all the stars were laughing when you look at the sky at night... You will have stars that can laugh!"

And he laughed again. "And when your sorrow is comforted, you will be happy that you have known me. You will always be my friend. You will want to laugh with me. And you will sometimes open your window for that pleasure... And your friends will be surely surprised to see you laughing as you look up at the sky! Then you will say to them, 'Yes, the stars always make me laugh!' And they will think you are crazy. It will be a very mean trick that I will have played on you..."
And he laughed again. "Instead of stars, it will be like I had given you a great number of little bells that knew how to laugh..." And he laughed again.

Then he quickly became serious:

"Tonight—you know... Do not come."

"I shall not leave you," I said.

"I shall look as if I were suffering. I shall look a little as if I were dying. It is like that. Do not come to see that. It is not worth the trouble..."

"I shall not leave you."

But he was worried. "I tell you—it is also because of the snake. The snake must not bite you. Snakes are unkind creatures. This one might bite you just for fun..."

"I shall not leave you." But a thought came to comfort him:

"It is true that snakes have no more poison for a second bite."

That night I did not see him set out on his way. He got away from me without making a sound. When I succeeded in catching up with him, he was walking along with a quick and steady step. He said to me simply:

"Ah! You are there..."

And he took me by the hand, but he was still worrying.

"It was wrong of you to come. You will suffer. I shall look as if I were dead, but that will not be true..."

I said nothing.

"You understand... it is too far. I cannot carry this body. It is too heavy."

I said nothing.

"But it will be like an old empty shell. There is nothing sad about old shells..."
I said nothing.

He was a little discouraged. But he made one more effort:
"You know, it will be very nice. I shall look at the stars, too. All the stars will be wells with an old well-wheel. All the stars will pour out fresh water for me to drink..."
I said nothing.

"That will be so interesting! You will have five hundred million little bells, and I shall have five hundred million springs of fresh water..." And he too said nothing more, because he was crying...

"Here it is. Let me go on by myself." And he sat down because he was afraid. Then he said, again:

"You know—my flower... I am responsible for her. And she is so weak! She is so naive! She has four thorns to protect herself against all the world..."

I too sat down, because I was not able to stand up any longer.

"There now-that is all..." He paused a little; then, he got up. He took one step. I could not move. There was nothing but a flash of yellow close to his ankle. He didn't move for an instant. He did not cry out. He fell as gently as a tree falls. There was not even any sound because of the sand.

Chapter 27

And now six years have already gone by... I have never yet told this story. The friends who met me on my return were pleased to see me alive. I was sad, but I told them:

"I am tired."

Now my sorrow is comforted a little, but not completely. I know that he did go back to his planet because I did not find his body in the early morning. It was not such a heavy body... and at night I love to listen to the stars. They are like five hundred million little bells...

But there is one strange thing... when I drew the mask for the little prince, I forgot to add the leather strap to it. He would never have been able to fasten it on his sheep. So now I keep wondering: what is happening on his planet? Perhaps the sheep has eaten the flower...

At one time, I say to myself:

"Surely not! The little prince shuts his flower under her glass cup every night and he watches over his sheep very carefully..." Then I am happy. And there is sweetness in the laughter of all the stars. But at another time, I say to myself:

"At some moment, he forgot the glass cup, or the sheep got out without making any noise in the night..." And then the little bells are changed to tears...

Here is a great mystery. For you who also love the little prince, and for me, nothing can be the same if a sheep we never saw has eaten a rose. Did he eat it? Yes or no... Look up at the sky. Ask yourselves: is it yes or no? You will see how everything changes... and grown-up will never understand that this is a matter of so much importance!

This is the loveliest and saddest landscape in the world. It is the same as that on the previous page, but I have drawn it again to impress it on your memory. It is here that the little prince appeared on Earth and disappeared.

Look at it carefully, so that you will be sure to remember it in case you travel someday to the African desert. And, if you should come upon this spot, please do not hurry on. Then, if a little man appears who laughs and has golden hair, you will know who he is. If this should happen, send me word that he has come back.

이제 다 왔습니다.

당신은 벌써 어린 왕자 원서를 3~4번 읽었습니다.

이제, 자신 있게 어린 왕자를 원문을 읽어 보세요.

읽다가 모르는 단어가 나오면 다시 Level 4로 내려가서

해당 문단을 읽어보세요. 몰랐던 단어 뜻을 쉽게 유추할 수 있습니다.

You are almost there!

You have now read The Little Prince in English three to four times.

Now, try to read the original version of The Little Prince with confidence.

If there are words that you do not know, read the corresponding paragraph

written in the Level 4 book.

You will easily be able to infer the meaning.

LEVEL 5

"The desert is beautiful," the little prince added.

And that was true. I have always loved the desert.
One sits down on a desert sand dune, sees nothing, hears nothing.
    Yet through the silence something throbs, and gleams...

"What makes the desert beautiful," said the little prince, "is that somewhere it
hides a well..."

I was astonished by a sudden understanding of that mysterious radiation of the
sands. The desert is beautiful because there is water cannot see.

The Little Prince
THE ORIGINAL TEXT

Chapter 1

Once when I was six years old, I saw a magnificent picture in a book, called True Stories from Nature, about the primeval forest. It was a picture of a boa constrictor in the act of swallowing an animal. Here is a copy of the drawing.

In the book, it said:

"Boa constrictors swallow their prey whole, without chewing it. After that, they are not able to move, and they sleep through the six months that they need for digestion."

I pondered deeply, then, over the adventures of the jungle. And after some work with a colored pencil, I succeeded in making my first drawing. My Drawing Number One. It looked like this:

first drawing

I showed my masterpiece to the grown-ups and asked them whether the drawing frightened them. But they answered:

"Frighten? Why should anyone be frightened by a hat?"

My drawing was not a picture of a hat. It was a picture of a boa constrictor digesting an elephant. But since the grown-ups were not able to understand it, I made another drawing: I drew the inside of the boa constrictor so that the grown-ups could see it clearly. They always need to have things explained. My Drawing Number Two looked like this:

drawing No.2

The grown-ups' response, this time, was to advise me to lay aside my drawings of boa constrictors, whether from the inside or the outside, and devote myself instead to geography, history, arithmetic, and grammar. That is why, at the age of six, I gave up what might have been a magnificent career as a painter. I had been disheartened by the failure of my Drawing Number One and my Drawing Number Two. Grown-ups never understand anything by themselves, and it is tiresome for children to be always and forever explaining things to them.

So then I chose another profession and learned to pilot airplanes. I have flown a little over all parts of the world, and it is true that geography has been very useful to me. At a glance, I can distinguish China from Arizona. If one gets lost in the night, such knowledge is valuable.

In the course of this life, I have had a great many encounters with a great many people who have been concerned with matters of consequence. I have lived a great deal among grown-ups. I have seen them intimately, close at hand. And that hasn't much improved my opinion of them.

Whenever I met one of them who seemed to me at all clear-sighted, I tried the experiment of showing him my Drawing Number One, which I have always kept. I would try to find out, so, if this was a person of true understanding. But, whoever it was, he, or she, would always say:

"That is a hat."

Then I would never talk to that person about boa constrictors, or primeval forests, or stars. I would bring myself down to his level. I would talk to him about bridge, and golf, and politics, and neckties. And the grown-up would be greatly pleased to have met such a sensible man.

Chapter 2

So I lived my life alone, without anyone that I could really talk to, until I had an accident with my plane in the Desert of Sahara, six years ago.

Something was broken in my engine. And as I had with me neither a mechanic nor any passengers, I set myself to attempt the difficult repairs all alone. It was a question of life or death for me: I had scarcely enough drinking water to last a week.

The first night, then, I went to sleep on the sand, a thousand miles from any human habitation. I was more isolated than a shipwrecked sailor on a raft in the middle of the ocean. Thus you can imagine my amazement, at sunrise, when I was awakened by an odd little voice. It said:

"If you please—draw me a sheep!"

"What!"

"Draw me a sheep!"

I jumped to my feet, completely thunderstruck. I blinked my eyes hard. I looked carefully all around me. And I saw a most extraordinary small person, who stood there examining me with great seriousness. Here you may see the best portrait that, later, I was able to make of him.

But my drawing is certainly very much less charming

Here you may see the best portrait that later, I was able to make of him.

than its model. That, however, is not my fault. The grown-ups discouraged me in my painter's career when I was six years old, and I never learned to draw anything, except boas from the outside and boas from the inside.

Now I stared at this sudden apparition with my eyes fairly starting out of my head in astonishment. Remember, I had crashed in the desert a thousand miles from any inhabited region.

And yet my little man seemed neither to be straying uncertainly among the sands nor to be fainting from fatigue or hunger or thirst or fear. Nothing about him gave any suggestion of a child lost in the middle of the desert, a thousand miles from any human habitation.

When at last I was able to speak, I said to him:

"But—what are you doing here?"

And in answer he repeated, very slowly, as if he were speaking of a matter of great consequence:

"If you please—draw me a sheep..."

When a mystery is too overpowering, one dare not disobey. Absurd as it might seem to me, a thousand miles from any human habitation and in danger of death, I took out of my pocket a sheet of paper and my fountain-pen.

But then I remembered how my studies had been concentrated on geography, history, arithmetic, and grammar, and I told the little chap (a little crossly, too) that

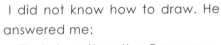

I did not know how to draw. He answered me:

"That doesn't matter. Draw me a sheep..."

But I had never drawn a sheep. So I drew for him one of the two pictures I had drawn so often. It was that of the boa constrictor from the outside.

And I was astounded to hear the little fellow greet it with, "No, no, no! I do not want an elephant inside a boa constrictor. A boa

constrictor is a very dangerous creature, and an elephant is very cumbersome. Where I live, everything is very small. What I need is a sheep. Draw me a sheep."

So then I made a drawing. He looked at it carefully, then he said:

"No. This sheep is already very sickly. Make me another."
So I made another drawing. My friend smiled gently and indulgently.

"You see yourself," he said, "that this is not a sheep. This is a ram. It has horns.

So then I did my drawing over once more. But it was rejected too, just like the others. "This one is too old. I want a sheep that will live a long time."

By this time my patience was exhausted because I was in a hurry to start taking my engine apart. So I tossed off this drawing. And I threw out an explanation with it. "This is only his box. The sheep you asked for is inside."

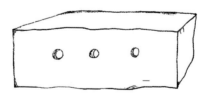

I was very surprised to see a light break over the face of my young judge:

"That is exactly the way I wanted it! Do you think that this sheep will have to have a great deal of grass?"

"Why?"

"Because where I live everything is very small..."

"There will surely be enough grass for him," I said. "It is a very small sheep that I have given you."

He bent his head over the drawing.

"Not so small that—Look! He has gone to sleep..."

And that is how I made the acquaintance of the little prince.

Chapter 3

It took me a long time to learn where he came from. The little prince, who asked me so many questions, never seemed to hear the ones I asked him. It was from words dropped by chance that, little by little, everything was revealed to me.

The first time he saw my airplane, for instance (I shall not draw my airplane; that would be much too complicated for me), he asked me:

"What is that object?"

"That is not an object. It flies. It is an airplane. It is my airplane." And I was proud to have him learn that I could fly.

He cried out, then: "What! You dropped down from the sky?"

"Yes," I answered modestly.

"Oh! That is funny!" And the little prince broke into a lovely peal of laughter, which irritated me very much. I like my misfortunes to be taken seriously.

Then he added: "So you, too, come from the sky! Which is your planet?"
At that moment I caught a gleam of light in the impenetrable mystery of his presence; and I demanded, abruptly:

"Do you come from another planet?" But he did not reply.

He tossed his head gently, without taking his eyes from my plane:
"It is true that on that you can't have come from very far away..." And he sank into a reverie, which lasted a long time. Then, taking my sheep out of his pocket, he buried himself in the contemplation of his treasure. You can imagine how my curiosity was aroused by this half-confidence about the "other planets." I made a great effort, therefore, to find out more on this subject.

"My little man, where do you come from? What is this 'where I live,' of which you speak? Where do you want to take your sheep?" After a reflective silence, he answered:

"The thing that is so good about the box you have given me is that at night, he can ."

"That is so. And if you are good, I will give you a string, too, so that you can tie him during the day, and a post to tie him to."

But the little prince seemed shocked by this offer:

"Tie him! What a queer idea!"

"But if you don't tie him," I said, "he will wander off somewhere, and get lost." My friend broke into another peal of laughter:

"But where do you think he would go?"

"Anywhere. Straight ahead of him." Then the little prince said, earnestly:

"That doesn't matter. Where I live, everything is so small!" And, with perhaps a hint of sadness, he added: "Straight ahead of him, nobody can go very far..."

Chapter 4

I had thus learned a second fact of great importance: this was that the planet the little prince came from was scarcely any larger than a house! But that did not really surprise me much. I knew very well that in addition to the great planets—such as the Earth, Jupiter, Mars, Venus—to which we have given names, there are also hundreds of others, some of which are so small that one has a hard time seeing them through the telescope.

When an astronomer discovers one of these, he does not give it a name, but only a number. He might call it, for example, "Asteroid 325." I have serious reason to believe that the planet from which the little prince came is the asteroid known as B-612.

This asteroid has only once been seen through the telescope. That was by a Turkish astronomer, in 1909. On making his discovery, the astronomer had presented it to the International Astronomical Congress, in a great demonstration. But he was in Turkish costume, and so nobody would believe what he said. Grown-ups are like that...

Fortunately, however, for the reputation of Asteroid B-612, a Turkish dictator made a law that his subjects, under pain of death, should change to European costume. So in 1920, the astronomer gave his demonstration all over again, dressed with impressive style and elegance. And this time everybody accepted his report.

If I have told you these details about the asteroid and made a note of its number for you, it is on account of the grown-ups and their ways. When you tell them that you have made a new friend, they never ask you any questions about essential matters. They never say to you, "What does his voice sound like? What games does he love best? Does he collect butterflies?" Instead, they demand: "How old is he? How many brothers has he? How much does he weigh? How much money does his father make?" Only from these figures do they think they have learned anything about him.

If you were to say to the grown-ups: "I saw a beautiful house made of rosy brick, with geraniums in the windows and doves on the roof," they would not be able to get any idea of that house at all. You would have to say to them: "I saw a house that cost $20,000." Then they would exclaim: "Oh, what a pretty house that is!"

Just so, you might say to them: "The proof that the little prince existed is that he was charming, that he laughed, and that he was looking for a sheep. If anybody wants a sheep, that is a proof that he exists." And what good would it do to tell them that? They would shrug their shoulders and treat you like a child.

But if you said to them: "The planet he came from is Asteroid

B-612," then they would be convinced, and leave you in peace from their questions. They are like that. One must not hold it against them. Children should always show great forbearance toward grown-up people. But certainly, for us who understand life, figures are a matter of indifference.

I should have liked to begin this story in the fashion of the fairy-tales. I should have like to say: "Once upon a time there was a little prince who lived on a planet that was scarcely any bigger than himself, and who had need of a sheep..." To those who understand life, that would have given a much greater air of truth to my story. For I do not want anyone to read my book carelessly.

I have suffered too much grief in setting down these memories. Six years have already passed since my friend went away from me, with his sheep. If I try to describe him here, it is to make sure that I shall not forget him. To forget a friend is sad. Not everyone has had a friend. And if I forget him, I may become like the grown-ups who are no longer interested in anything but figures...

It is for that purpose, again, that I have bought a box of paints and some pencils. It is hard to take up drawing again at my age, when I have never made any pictures except those of the boa constrictor from the outside and the boa constrictor from the inside, since I was six.

I shall certainly try to make my portraits as true to life as possible. But I am not at all sure of success. One drawing goes along all right, and another has no resemblance to its subject. I make some errors, too, in the little prince's height: in one place he is too tall and in another too short. And I feel some doubts about the color of his costume. So I fumble along as best I can, now good, now bad, and I hope generally fair-to-middling.

In certain more important details, I shall make mistakes, also. But that is something that will not be my fault. My friend never explained anything to me. He thought, perhaps, that I was like himself. But I, alas, do not know how to see sheep through the walls of boxes. Perhaps I am a little like the grown-ups. I have had to grow old.

Chapter 5

As each day passed, I would learn, in our talk, something about the little prince's planet, his departure from it, his journey. The information would come very slowly, as it might chance to fall from his thoughts. It was in this way that I heard, on the third day, about the catastrophe of the baobabs. This time, once more, I had the sheep to thank for it.

For the little prince asked me abruptly—as if seized by a grave doubt—"It is true, isn't it, that sheep eat little bushes?"
"Yes, that is true."
"Ah! I am glad!"
I did not understand why it was so important that sheep should eat little bushes.

But the little prince added: "Then it follows that they also eat baobabs?"
I pointed out to the little prince that baobabs were not little bushes, but, on the contrary, trees as big as castles; and that even if he took a whole herd of elephants away with him, the herd would not eat up one single baobab.

The idea of the herd of elephants made the little prince laugh. "We would have to put them one on top of the other," he said.
But he made a wise comment:

"Before they grow so big, the baobabs start out by being little."

"That is strictly correct," I said. "But why do you want the sheep to eat the little baobabs?"

He answered me at once, "Oh, come, come!" as if he were speaking of something that was self-evident.

And I was obliged to make a great mental effort to solve this problem, without any assistance. Indeed, as I learned, there were on the planet where the little prince lived— as on all planets—good plants and bad plants. In consequence, there were good seeds from good plants and bad seeds from bad plants. But seeds are invisible. They sleep deep in the heart of the earth's darkness until someone among them is seized with the desire to awaken. Then this little seed will stretch itself and begin—timidly at first—to push a charming little sprig inoffensively upward toward the sun. If it is only a sprout of radish or the sprig of a rose-bush, one would let it grow wherever it might wish. But when it is a bad plant, one must destroy it as soon as possible, the very first instant that one recognizes it.

Now there were some terrible seeds on the planet that was the home of the little prince; and these were the seeds of the baobab. The soil of that planet was infested with them. A baobab is something you will never, never be able to get rid of if you attend to it too late. It spreads over the entire planet. It bores clear through it with its roots. And if the planet is too small, and the baobabs are too many, they split it into pieces...

"It is a question of discipline," the little prince said to me later on. "When you've finished your own toilet in the morning, then it is time to attend to the toilet of your planet, just so, with the greatest care. You must see to it that you pull up regularly all the baobabs, at the very first moment when they can be distinguished from the rosebushes which they resemble so closely in their earliest youth. It is very tedious work," the little prince added, "but very easy."

The baobabs.

And one day he said to me: "You ought to make a beautiful drawing so that the children where you live can see exactly how all this is. That would be very useful to them if they were to travel someday. Sometimes," he added, "there is no harm in putting off a piece of work until another day. But when it is a matter of baobabs, that always means a catastrophe. I knew a planet that was inhabited by a lazy man. He neglected three little bushes..."

So, as the little prince described it to me, I have made a drawing of that planet. I do not much like to take the tone of a moralist. But the danger of the baobabs is so little understood, and such considerable risks would be run by anyone who might get lost on an asteroid, that for once I am breaking through my reserve. "Children," I say plainly, "watch out for the baobabs!"

My friends, like myself, have been skirting this danger for a long time, without ever knowing it; and so it is for them that I have worked so hard over this drawing. The lesson which I pass on by this means is worth all the trouble it has cost me.

Perhaps you will ask me, "Why are there no other drawing in this book as magnificent and impressive as this drawing of the baobabs?" The reply is simple. I have tried. But with the others, I have not been successful. When I made the drawing of the baobabs, I was carried beyond myself by the inspiring force of urgent necessity.

Chapter 6

Oh, little prince! Bit by bit I came to understand the secrets of your sad little life... For a long time, you had found your only entertainment in the quiet pleasure of looking at the sunset.

I learned that new detail on the morning of the fourth day when you said to me:

"I am very fond of sunsets. Come, let us go look at a sunset now."

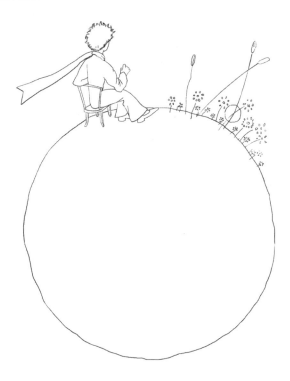

"But we must wait," I said.

"Wait? For what?"

"For the sunset. We must wait until it is time."

At first, you seemed to be very much surprised. And then you laughed to yourself. You said to me:

"I am always thinking that I am at home!"

Just so. Everybody knows that when it is noon in the United States, the sun is setting over France. If you could fly to France in one minute, you could go straight into the sunset, right from noon. Unfortunately, France is too far away for that. But on your tiny planet, my little prince, all you need do is move your chair a few steps. You can see the day end and the twilight falling whenever you like...

"One day," you said to me, "I saw the sunset forty-four times!" And a little later you added: "You know-one loves the sunset when one is so sad..."

"Were you so sad, then?" I asked, "On the day of the forty-four sunsets?"

But the little prince made no reply.

Chapter 7

On the fifth day-again, as always, it was thanks to the sheep-the secret of the little prince's life was revealed to me. Abruptly, without anything to lead up to it, and as if the question had been born of long and silent meditation on his problem, he demanded:

"A sheep—if it eats little bushes, does it eat flowers, too?"

"A sheep," I answered, "eats anything it finds in its reach."

"Even flowers that have thorns?"

"Yes, even flowers that have thorns."

"Then the thorns—what use are they?"

I did not know. At that moment, I was very busy trying to unscrew a bolt that had got stuck in my engine. I was very much worried, for it was becoming clear to me that the breakdown of my plane was extremely serious. And I had so little drinking-water left that I had to fear for the worst.

"The thorns—what use are they?" The little prince never let go of a question, once he had asked it. As for me, I was upset over that bolt. And I answered with the first thing that came into my head:

"The thorns are of no use at all. Flowers have thorns just for spite!"

"Oh!" There was a moment of complete silence. Then the little prince flashed back at me, with a kind of resentfulness:

"I don't believe you! Flowers are weak creatures. They are naive. They reassure themselves as best they can. They believe that their thorns are terrible weapons..."

I did not answer. At that instant, I was saying to myself:

"If this bolt still won't turn, I am going to knock it out with the hammer."

Again the little prince disturbed my thoughts:

"And you actually believe that the flowers—"

"Oh, no!" I cried. "No, no, no! I don't believe anything. I answered you with the first thing that came into my head. Don't you see—I am very busy with matters of consequence!"

He stared at me, thunderstruck. "Matters of consequence!" He looked at me there, with my hammer in my hand, my fingers black with engine-grease, bending down over an

 object which seemed to him extremely ugly...

"You talk just like the grown-ups!"

That made me a little ashamed. But he went on, relentlessly:

"You mix everything up together... You confuse everything..." He was really very angry. He tossed his golden curls in the breeze.

"I know a planet where there is a certain red-faced gentleman. He has never smelled a flower. He has never looked at a star. He has never loved anyone. He has never done anything in his life but adds up figures. And all day he says over and over, just like you: 'I am busy with matters of consequence!' And that makes him swell up with pride. But he is not a man, he is a mushroom!"

"A what?"

"A mushroom!" The little prince was now white with rage.

"The flowers have been growing thorns for millions of years. For millions of years, the sheep have been eating them just the same. And is it not a matter of consequence to try to understand why the flowers go to so much trouble to grow thorns which are never of any use to them? Is the warfare between the sheep and the flowers not important? Is this not of more consequence than a fat red-faced gentleman's sums?"

"And if I know—I, myself—one flower which is unique in the world, which grows nowhere but on my planet, but which one little sheep can destroy in a single bite some morning, without even noticing what he is doing-Oh! You think that is not important!"

His face turned from white to red as he continued:

"If someone loves a flower, of which just one single blossom grows in all the millions and millions of stars, it is enough to make him happy just to look at the stars. He can say to himself, 'Somewhere, my flower is there...' But if the sheep eats the flower, in one moment all his stars will be darkened... And you think that is not important!"

He could not say anything more. His words were choked by sobbing. The night had fallen. I had let my tools drop from my hands. Of what moment now was my hammer, my bolt, or thirst, or death? On one star, one planet, my planet, the Earth, there was a little prince to be comforted.

I took him in my arms and rocked him. I said to him:

"The flower that you love is not in danger. I will draw you a muzzle for your sheep. I will draw you a railing to put around your flower. I will—" I did not know what to say to him. I felt awkward and blundering. I did not know how I could reach him, where I could overtake him and go on hand in hand with him once more. It is such a secret place, the land of tears.

Chapter 8

I soon learned to know this flower better. On the little prince's planet, the flowers had always been very simple. They had only one ring of petals; they took up no room at all; they were a trouble to nobody. One morning they would appear in the grass, and by night they would have faded peacefully away.

But one day, from a seed blown from no one, knew where a new flower had come up; and the little prince had watched very closely over this small sprout which was not like any other small sprouts on his planet. It might, you see, have been a new kind of baobab.

The shrub soon stopped growing and began to get ready to produce a flower. The little prince, who was present at the first appearance of a huge bud, felt at once that some sort of miraculous apparition must emerge from it. But the flower was not satisfied to complete the preparations for her beauty in the shelter of her green chamber.

She chose her colors with the greatest care. She dressed herself slowly. She adjusted her petals one by one. She did not wish to go out into the world all rumpled, like the field poppies. It was only in the full radiance of her beauty that she wished to appear. Oh, yes! She was a coquettish creature! And her mysterious adornment lasted for days and days.

Then one morning, exactly at sunrise, she suddenly showed herself.
And, after working with all this painstaking precision, she yawned and said:

"Ah! I am scarcely awake. I beg that you will excuse me. My petals are still all disarranged..."

But the little prince could not restrain his admiration:

"Oh! How beautiful you are!"

"Am I not?" the flower responded, sweetly. "And I was born at the same moment as the sun..."
The little prince could guess easily enough that she was not any too modest—but how moving—and exciting—she was!

"I think it is time for breakfast," she added an instant later. "If you would have the kindness to think of my needs—"
And the little prince, completely abashed, went to look for a sprinkling-can of fresh water. So, he tended the flower.
So, too, she began very quickly to torment him with her vanity—which was, if the truth be known, a little difficult to deal with.

One day, for instance, when she was speaking of her four thorns, she said to the little prince:

"Let the tigers come with their claws!"

"There are no tigers on my planet," the little prince objected. "And, anyway, tigers do not eat weeds."

"I am not a weed," the flower replied, sweetly.

"Please excuse me..."

"I am not at all afraid of tigers," she went on, "but I have a horror of drafts. I suppose you wouldn't have a screen for me?"

"A horror of drafts—that is bad luck, for a plant," remarked the little prince, and added to himself, "This flower is a very complex creature..."

"At night I want you to put me under a glass globe. It is very cold where you live. In the place, I came from..." But she interrupted herself at that point. She had come in the form of a seed. She could not have known anything of any other worlds. Embarrassed over having let herself be caught on the verge of such a naive untruth, she coughed two or three times, in order to put the little prince in the wrong.

"The screen?"

"I was just going to look for it when you spoke to me..."

Then she forced her cough a little more so that he should suffer from remorse just the same. So the little prince, in spite of all the goodwill that was inseparable from his love, had soon come to doubt her. He had taken seriously words which were without importance, and it made him very unhappy.

"I ought not to have listened to her," he confided to me

one day. "One never ought to listen to the flowers. One should simply look at them and breathe their fragrance. Mine perfumed all my planet. But I did not know how to take pleasure in all her grace. This tale of claws, which disturbed me so much, should only have filled my heart with tenderness and pity."

And he continued his confidences:

"The fact is that I did not know how to understand anything! I ought to have judged by deeds and not by words. She cast her fragrance and her radiance over me. I ought never to have run away from her... I ought to have guessed all the affection that lay behind her poor little stratagems. Flowers are so inconsistent! But I was too young to know how to love her..."

Chapter 9

I believe that for his escape he took advantage of the migration of a flock of wild birds. On the morning of his departure, he put his planet in perfect order. He carefully cleaned out his active volcanoes. He possessed two active volcanoes; and they were very convenient for heating his breakfast in the morning.

He also had one volcano that was extinct. But, as he said, "One never knows!" So he cleaned out the extinct volcano, too. If they are well cleaned out, volcanoes burn slowly and steadily, without any eruptions. Volcanic eruptions are like fires in a chimney. On our earth, we are obviously much too small to clean out our volcanoes. That is why they bring no end of trouble upon us.

The little prince also pulled up, with a certain sense of dejection, the last little shoots of the baobabs. He believed that he would never want to return. But on this last morning, all these familiar tasks seemed very precious to him. And when he watered the flower for the last time and prepared to place her under the shelter of her glass globe, he realized that he was very close to tears.

"Goodbye," he said to the flower.
But she made no answer.
"Goodbye," he said again.

He carefully cleaned out his active volcanoes.

The flower coughed. But it was not because she had a cold. "I have been silly," she said to him, at last. "I ask your forgiveness. Try to be happy..."

He was surprised by this absence of reproaches. He stood there all bewildered, the glass globe held arrested in mid-air. He did not understand this quiet sweetness.

"Of course I love you," the flower said to him. "It is my fault that you have not known it all the while. That is of no importance. But you, you have been just as foolish as I. Try to be happy... Let the glass globe be. I don't want it anymore."

"But the wind..."

"My cold is not so bad as all that... The cool night air will do me good. I am a flower."

"But the animals..."

"Well, I must endure the presence of two or three caterpillars if I wish to become acquainted with the butterflies. It seems that they are very beautiful. And if not the butterflies and the caterpillars who will call upon me? You will be far away..."

"As for the large animals, I am not at all afraid of any of them. I have my claws." And, naively, she showed her four thorns. Then she added:

"Don't linger like this. You have decided to go away. Now go!" For she did not want him to see, her crying. She was such a proud flower...

Chapter 10

He found himself in the neighborhood of the asteroids 325, 326, 327, 328, 329, and 330. He began, therefore, by visiting them, in order to add to his knowledge.

The first of them was inhabited by a king. Clad in royal purple and ermine, he was seated upon a throne which was at the same time both simple and majestic. "Ah! Here is a subject," exclaimed the king, when he saw the little prince coming.

And the little prince asked himself:
"How could he recognize me when he had never seen me before?" He did not know how the world is simplified for kings. To them, all men are subjects.
"Approach, so that I may see you better," said the king, who felt consumingly proud of being, at last, a king over somebody.

The little prince looked everywhere to find a place to sit down, but the entire planet was crammed and obstructed by the king's magnificent ermine robe. So he remained standing upright.

And, since he was tired, he yawned.
"It is contrary to etiquette to yawn in the presence of a king," the monarch said to him. "I forbid you to do so."

"I can't help it. I can't stop myself," replied the little prince, thoroughly embarrassed. "I have come on a long journey, and I have had no sleep…"

"Ah, then," the king said. "I order you to yawn. It is years since I have seen anyone yawning. Yawns, to me, are objects of curiosity. Come, now! Yawn again! It is an order."

"That frightens me… I cannot, anymore…" murmured the little prince, now completely abashed.

"Hum! Hum!" replied the king. "Then I—I order you sometimes to yawn and sometimes to—" He sputtered a little, and seemed vexed. For what the king fundamentally insisted upon was that his authority should be respected. He tolerated no disobedience. He was an absolute monarch.

But, because he was a very good man, he made his orders reasonable. "If I ordered a general," he would say, by way of example, "if I ordered a general to change himself into a sea bird, and if the general did not obey me, that would not be the fault of the general. It would be my fault."

"May I sit down?" came now a timid inquiry from the little prince.

"I order you to do so," the king answered him, and majestically gathered in a fold of his ermine mantle.

But the little prince was wondering… The planet was tiny. Over what could this king really rule?

"Sire," he said to him, "I beg that you will excuse my asking you a question—"

"I order you to ask me a question," the king hastened to assure him.

"Sire, over what do you rule?"

"Over everything," said the king, with magnificent simplicity.

"Over everything?"

The king made a gesture, which took in his planet, the other planets, and all the stars.

"Over all that?" asked the little prince.

"Over all that," the king answered.

For his rule was not only absolute: it was also universal.

"And the stars obey you?"

"Certainly they do," the king said. "They obey instantly. I do not permit insubordination."

Such power was a thing for the little prince to marvel at. If he had been master of such complete authority, he would have been able to watch the sunset, not forty-four times in one day, but seventy-two, or even a hundred, or even two hundred times, without ever having to move his chair.

And because he felt a bit sad as he remembered his little planet which he had forsaken, he plucked up his courage to ask the king a favor: "I should like to see a sunset... Do me that kindness... Order the sun to set..."

"If I ordered a general to fly from one flower to another

like a butterfly, or to write a tragic drama, or to change himself into a sea bird, and if the general did not carry out the order that he had received, which one of us would be in the wrong?" the king demanded. "The general, or myself?"

"You," said the little prince firmly.

"Exactly. One must require from each one the duty which each one can perform," the king went on. "Accepted authority rests first of all on reason. If you ordered your people to go and throw themselves into the sea, they would rise up in revolution. I have the right to require obedience because my orders are reasonable."

"Then my sunset?" the little prince reminded him: for he never forgot a question once he had asked it.

"You shall have your sunset. I shall command it. But, according to my science of government, I shall wait until conditions are favorable."

"When will that be?" inquired the little prince.

"Hum! Hum!" replied the king; and before saying anything else, he consulted a bulky almanac. "Hum! Hum! That will be about-about-that will be this evening about twenty minutes to eight. And you will see how well I am obeyed!"

The little prince yawned. He was regretting his lost sunset. And then, too, he was already beginning to be a little bored. "I have nothing more to do here," he said to the king. "So I shall set out on my way again."

"Do not go," said the king, who was very proud of having a subject. "Do not go. I will make you a Minister!"

"Minister of what?"

"Minster of-of Justice!"

"But there is nobody here to judge!"

"We do not know that," the king said to him. "I have not yet made a complete tour of my kingdom. I am very old. There is no room here for a carriage. And it tires me to walk."

"Oh, but I have looked already!" said the little prince, turning around to give one more glance to the other side of the planet. On that side, as on this, there was nobody at all...

"Then you shall judge yourself," the king answered, "that is the most difficull thing of all. It is much more difficult to judge oneself than to judge others. If you succeed in judging yourself rightly, then you are indeed a man of true wisdom."

"Yes," said the little prince, "but I can judge myself anywhere. I do not need to live on this planet.

"Hum! Hum!" said the king. "I have good reason to believe that somewhere on my planet there is an old rat. I hear him at night. You can judge this old rat. From time to time, you will condemn him to death. Thus his life will depend on your justice. But you will pardon him on each occasion; for he must be treated thriftily. He is the only one we have."

"I," replied the little prince, "do not like to condemn anyone to death. And now I think I will go on my way."

"No," said the king.

But the little prince, having now completed his preparations for departure, had no wish to grieve the old monarch.

"If Your Majesty wishes to be promptly obeyed," he said, "he should be able to give me a reasonable order. He should be able, for example, to order me to be gone by the end of one minute. It seems to me that conditions are favorable..."

As the king made no answer, the little prince hesitated a moment. Then, with a sigh, he took his leave.

"I make you my Ambassador," the king called out, hastily. He had a magnificent air of authority.

"The grown-ups are very strange," the little prince said to himself, as he continued on his journey.

Chapter 11

The second planet was inhabited by a conceited man. "Ah! Ah! I am about to receive a visit from an admirer!" he exclaimed from afar when he first saw the little prince coming. For, to conceited men, all other men are admirers.

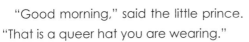

"Good morning," said the little prince. "That is a queer hat you are wearing."

"It is a hat for salutes," the conceited man replied. "It is to raise in salute when people acclaim me. Unfortunately, nobody at all ever passes this way."

"Yes?" said the little prince, who did not understand what the conceited man was talking about.

"Clap your hands, one against the other," the conceited man now directed him. The little prince clapped his hands. The conceited man raised his hat in a modest salute.

"This is more entertaining than the visit to the king," the little prince said to himself.

And he began again to clap his hands, one against the other. The conceited man again raised his hat in salute. After five minutes of this exercise, the little prince grew tired of the game's monotony.

"And what should one do to make the hat come down?" he asked.

But the conceited man did not hear him. Conceited people never hear anything but praise.

"Do you really admire me very much?" he demanded of the little prince.

"What does that mean—'admire'?"

"To admire means that you regard me as the handsomest, the best-dressed, the richest, and the most intelligent man on this planet."

"But you are the only man on your planet!"

"Do me this kindness. Admire me just the same."

"I admire you," said the little prince, shrugging his shoulders slightly, "but what is there in that to interest you so much?"

And the little prince went away. "The grown-ups are certainly very odd," he said to himself, as he continued on his journey.

Chapter 12

The next planet was inhabited by a tippler. This was a very short visit, but it plunged the little prince into deep dejection.

"What are you doing there?" he said to the tippler, whom he found settled down in silence before a collection of empty bottles and also a collection of full bottles.

"I am drinking," replied the tippler, with a lugubrious air.

"Why are you drinking?" demanded the little prince.

"So that I may forget," replied the tippler.

"Forget what?" inquired the little prince, who already was sorry for him.

"Forget that I am ashamed," the tippler confessed, hanging his head.

"Ashamed of what?" insisted the little prince, who wanted to help him.

"Ashamed of drinking!" The tippler brought his speech to an end and shut himself up in an impregnable silence.

And the little prince went away, puzzled. "The grown-ups are certainly very, very odd," he said to himself, as he continued on his journey.

Chapter 13

The fourth planet belonged to a businessman. This man was so much occupied that he did not even raise his head at the little prince's arrival. "Good morning," the little prince said to him. "Your cigarette has gone out."

"Three and two make five. Five and seven make twelve. Twelve and three make fifteen. Good morning. Fifteen and seven make twenty-two. Twenty-two and six make twenty-eight. I haven't time to light it again. Twenty-six and five make thirty-one. Phew! Then that makes five-hundred-and-one million, six-hundred-twenty-two-thousand, seven-hundred-thirty-one."

"Five hundred million what?" asked the little prince.

"Eh? Are you still there? Five-hundred-and-one million, I can't stop... I have so much to do! I am concerned with matters of consequence. I don't amuse myself with balderdash. Two and five make seven.

"Five-hundred-and-one million what?" repeated the little prince, who never in his life had let go of a question once he had asked it.

The businessman raised his head. "During the fifty-four years that I have inhabited this planet, I have been disturbed only three times. The first time was twenty-two years ago when some giddy goose fell from goodness knows where. He made the most frightful noise that resounded all over the place, and I made four mistakes in my addition."

"The second time, eleven years ago, I was disturbed by an attack of rheumatism. I don't get enough exercise. I have no time for loafing. The third time, well, this is it! I was saying, then, five-hundred-and-one millions—"

"Millions of what?" The businessman suddenly realized that there was no hope of being left in peace until he answered this question.

"Millions of those little objects," he said, "which one sometimes sees in the sky."

"Flies?"

"Oh, no. Little glittering objects."

"Bees?"

"Oh, no. Little golden objects that set lazy men to idle

dreaming. As for me, I am concerned with matters of consequence. There is no time for idle dreaming in my life."

"Ah! You mean the stars?"

"Yes, that's it. The stars."

"And what do you do with five-hundred millions of stars?"

"Five-hundred and-one million, six-hundred-twenty-two thousand, seven-hundred-thirty-one. I am concerned with matters of consequence: I am accurate."

"And what do you do with these stars?"

"What do I do with them?"

"Yes."

"Nothing. I own them."

"You own the stars?"

"Yes."

"But I have already seen a king who—"

"Kings do not own, they reign over. It is a very different matter."

"And what good does it do you to own the stars?"

"It does me the good of making me rich."

"And what good does it do you to be rich?"

"It makes it possible for me to buy more stars if any are discovered."

"This man," the little prince said to himself, "reasons a little like my poor tippler..." Nevertheless, he still had some more questions.

"How is it possible for one to own the stars?"

"To whom do they belong?" the businessman retorted, peevishly.

"I don't know. To nobody."

"Then they belong to me because I was the first person to think of it."

"Is that all that is necessary?"

"Certainly. When you find a diamond that belongs to nobody, it is yours. When you discover an island that belongs to nobody, it is yours. When you get an idea before anyone else, you take out a patent on it: it is yours. So with me: I own the stars because nobody else before me ever thought of owning them."

"Yes, that is true," said the little prince. "And what do you do with them?"

"I administer them," replied the businessman. "I count them and recount them. It is difficult. But I am a man who is naturally interested in matters of consequence."

The little prince was still not satisfied. "If I owned a silk scarf," he said, "I could put it around my neck and take it away with me. If I owned a flower, I could pluck that flower and take it away with me. But you cannot pluck the stars from heaven..."

"No. But I can put them in the bank."

"Whatever does that mean?"

"That means that I write the number of my stars on a little paper. And then I put this paper in a drawer and lock it with a key."

"And that is all?"

"That is enough," said the businessman.

"It is entertaining," thought the little prince. "It is rather poetic. But it is of no great consequence." On matters of consequence, the little prince had ideas which were very different from those of the grown-ups.

"I myself own a flower," he continued his conversation with the businessman, "which I water every day. I own three volcanoes, which I clean out every week (for I also clean out the one that is extinct; one never knows). It is of some use to my volcanoes, and it is of some use to my flower, that I own them."

"But you are of no use to the stars..." The businessman opened his mouth, but he found nothing to say in answer. And the little prince went away. "The grown-ups are certainly altogether extraordinary," he said simply, talking to himself as he continued on his journey.

Chapter 14

The fifth planet was very strange. It was the smallest of all. There was just enough room on it for a street lamp and a lamplighter. The little prince was not able to reach any explanation of the use of a street lamp and a lamplighter, somewhere in the heavens, on a planet which had no people, and not one house.

But he said to himself, nevertheless: "It may well be that this man is absurd. But he is not so absurd as the king, the conceited man, the businessman, and the tippler. For at least his work has some meaning."

"When he lights his street lamp, it is as if he brought one more star to life or one flower. When he puts out his lamp, he sends the flower, or the star, to sleep. That is a beautiful occupation. And since it is beautiful, it is truly useful."

When he arrived on the planet, he respectfully saluted the lamplighter. "Good morning. Why have you just put out your lamp?"
"Those are the orders," replied the lamplighter. "Good morning."

"What are the orders?"
"The orders are that I put out my lamp. Good evening."
And he lighted his lamp again.

"But why have you just lighted it again?"

"Those are the orders," replied the lamplighter.

"I do not understand," said the little prince.

"There is nothing to understand," said the lamplighter. "Orders are orders. Good morning." And he put out his lamp. Then he mopped his forehead with a handkerchief decorated with red squares.

I follow a terrible profession.

"I follow a terrible profession. In the old days it was reasonable. I put the lamp out in the morning, and in the evening, I lighted it again. I had the rest of the day for relaxation and the rest of the night for sleep."

"And the orders have been changed since that time?"

"The orders have not been changed," said the lamplighter. "That is the tragedy! From year to year, the planet has turned more rapidly, and the orders have not been changed!"

"Then what?" asked the little prince.

"Then-the planet now makes a complete turn every minute, and I no longer have a single second for repose. Once every minute I have to light my lamp and put it out!"

"That is very funny! A day lasts only one minute, here where you live!"

"It is not funny at all!" said the lamplighter. "While we have been talking together a month has gone by."

"A month?"

"Yes, a month. Thirty minutes. Thirty days. Good evening."

And he lighted his lamp again. As the little prince watched him, he felt that he loved this lamplighter who was so faithful to his orders. He remembered the sunsets which he himself had gone to seek, in other days, merely by pulling up his chair; and he wanted to help his friend.

"You know," he said, "I can tell you a way you can rest whenever you want to..."

"I always want to rest," said the lamplighter. For it is possible for a man to be faithful and lazy at the same time.

The little prince went on with his explanation: "Your planet is so small that three strides will take you all the way around it. To be always in the sunshine, you need only walk along rather slowly. When you want to rest, you will walk—and the day will last as long as you like."

"That doesn't do me much good," said the lamplighter.

"The one thing I love in life is to sleep."

"Then you're unlucky," said the little prince.

"I am unlucky," said the lamplighter. "Good morning." And he put out his lamp.

"That man," said the little prince to himself, as he continued farther on his journey, "that man would be scorned by all the others: by the king, by the conceited man, by the tippler, by the businessman. Nevertheless, he is the only one of them all who does not seem to me ridiculous. Perhaps that is because he is thinking of something else besides himself."

He breathed a sigh of regret, and said to himself, again: "That man is the only one of them all whom I could have made my friend. But his planet is indeed too small. There is no room on it for two people..." What the little prince did not dare confess was that he was sorry most of all to leave this planet, because it was blessed every day with 1440 sunsets!

Chapter 15

The sixth planet was ten times larger than the last one. It was inhabited by an old gentleman who wrote voluminous books. "Oh, look! Here is an explorer!" he exclaimed to himself when he saw the little prince coming.

The little prince sat down on the table and panted a little. He had already traveled so much and so far!

"Where do you come from?" the old gentleman said to him.

"What is that big book?" said the little prince. "What are you doing?"

"I am a geographer," said the old gentleman.

"What is a geographer?" asked the little prince.

"A geographer is a scholar who knows the location of all the seas, rivers, towns, mountains, and deserts."

"That is very interesting," said the little prince.

"Here, at last, is a man who has a real profession!" And he cast a look around him at the planet of the geographer. It was the most magnificent and stately planet that he had ever seen.

"Your planet is very beautiful," he said. "Has it any oceans?"

"I couldn't tell you," said the geographer.

"Ah!" The little prince was disappointed. "Has it any mountains?"

"I couldn't tell you," said the geographer.

"And towns, and rivers, and deserts?"

"I couldn't tell you that, either."

"But you are a geographer!"

"Exactly," the geographer said. "But I am not an explorer. I haven't a single explorer on my planet. It is not the geographer who goes out to count the towns, the rivers, the mountains, the seas, the oceans, and the deserts. The geographer is much too important to go loafing about. He does not leave his desk."

"But he receives the explorers in his study. He asks them questions, and he notes down what they recall of their travels. And if the recollections of anyone among them seem interesting to him, the geographer orders an inquiry into that explorer's moral character."

"Why is that?"

"Because an explorer who told lies would bring disaster on the books of the geographer. So would an explorer who drank too much."

"Why is that?" asked the little prince.

"Because intoxicated men see double. Then the geographer would note down two mountains in a place where there was only one."

"I know someone," said the little prince, "who would make a bad explorer."

"That is possible."

"Then, when the moral character of the explorer is shown to be good, an inquiry is ordered into his discovery."

"One goes to see it?"

"No. That would be too complicated. But one requires the explorer to furnish proofs. For example, if the discovery in question is that of a large mountain, one requires that large stones be brought back from it."

The geographer was suddenly stirred to excitement. "But you, you come from far away! You are an explorer! You shall describe your planet to me!" And, having opened his big register, the geographer sharpened his pencil. The recitals of explorers are put down first in pencil. One waits until the explorer has furnished proofs, before putting them down in ink.

"Well?" said the geographer expectantly.

"Oh, where I live," said the little prince, "it is not very interesting. It is all so small. I have three volcanoes. Two volcanoes are active, and the other is extinct. But one never knows."

"One never knows," said the geographer.

"I have also a flower."

"We do not record flowers," said the geographer.

"Why is that? The flower is the most beautiful thing on my planet!"

"We do not record them," said the geographer, "because they are ephemeral."

"What does that mean-ephemeral'?"

"Geographies," said the geographer, "are the books which, of all books, are most concerned with matters of consequence. They never become old fashioned. It is very rarely that a mountain changes its position. It is very rarely that an ocean empties itself of its waters. We write of eternal things."

"But extinct volcanoes may come to life again," the little prince interrupted. "What does that mean— 'ephemeral'?"

"Whether volcanoes are extinct or alive, it comes to the same thing for us," said the geographer. "The thing that matters to us is the mountain. It does not change."

"But what does that mean—'ephemeral'?" repeated the little prince, who never in his life had let go of a question, once he had asked it.

"It means, 'which is in danger of speedy disappearance.'"

"Is my flower in danger of speedy disappearance?"

"Certainly it is."

"My flower is ephemeral," the little prince said to himself, "and she has only four thorns to defend herself against the world. And I have left her on my planet, all alone!" That was his first moment of regret.

But he took courage once more. "What place would you advise me to visit now?" he asked.

"The planet Earth," replied the geographer. "It has a good reputation."

And the little prince went away, thinking of his flower.

Chapter 16

So then the seventh planet was the Earth. The Earth is not just an ordinary planet! One can count, there, 111 kings (not forgetting, to be sure, the African kings among them), 7000 geographers, 900,000 businessmen, 7,500,000 tipplers, 311,000,000 conceited men-that is to say, about 2,000,000,000 grown-ups.

To give you an idea of the size of the Earth, I will tell you that before the invention of electricity it was necessary to maintain, over the whole of the six continents, a veritable army of 462,511 lamplighters for the street lamps.

Seen from a slight distance, that would make a splendid spectacle. The movements of this army would be regulated like those of the ballet in the opera.

First would come the turn of the lamplighters of New Zealand and Australia. Having set their lamps alight, these would go off to sleep. Next, the lamplighters of China and Siberia would enter for their steps in the dance, and then they too would be waved back into the wings.

After that would come the turn of the lamplighters of Russia and the Indies; then those of Africa and Europe; then those of South America; then those of South America; then those of North America.

And never would they make a mistake in the order of their entry upon the stage. It would be magnificent. Only the man who was in charge of the single lamp at the North Pole, and his colleague who was responsible for the single lamp at the South Pole—only these two would live free from toil and care: they would be busy twice a year.

Chapter 17

When one wishes to play the wit, he sometimes wanders a little from the truth. I have not been altogether honest in what I have told you about the lamplighters. And I realize that I run the risk of giving a false idea of our planet to those who do not know it.

Men occupy a very small place upon the Earth. If the two billion inhabitants who people its surface were all to stand upright and somewhat crowded together, as they do for some big public assembly, they could easily be put into one public square twenty miles long and twenty miles wide. All humanity could be piled up on a small Pacific islet.

When the little prince arrived on the Earth, he was very much surprised not to see any people.

The grown-ups, to be sure, will not believe you when you tell them that. They imagine that they fill a great deal of space. They fancy themselves as important as the baobabs. You should advise them, then, to make their own calculations. They adore figures, and that will please them. But do not waste your time on this extra task. It is unnecessary. You have, I know, confidence in me.

When the little prince arrived on the Earth, he was very much surprised not to see any people. He was beginning to be afraid he had come to the wrong planet, when a coil of gold, the color of the moonlight, flashed across the sand.

"Good evening," said the little prince courteously.

"Good evening," said the snake.

"What planet is this on which I have come down?" asked the little prince.

"This is the Earth; this is Africa," the snake answered.

"Ah! Then there are no people on the Earth?"

"This is the desert. There are no people in the desert. The Earth is large," said the snake.

The little prince sat down on a stone and raised his eyes toward the sky. "I wonder," he said, "whether the stars are set alight in heaven so that one day each one of us may find his own again... Look at my planet. It is right there above us. But how far away it is!"

"It is beautiful," the snake said. "What has brought you here?"

"I have been having some trouble with a flower," said the little prince.

"Ah!" said the snake. And they were both silent.

"Where are the men?" the little prince, at last, took up the conversation again. "It is a little lonely in the desert..."

"It is also lonely among men," the snake said.

The little prince gazed at him for a long time. "You are a funny animal," he said at last. "You are no thicker than a finger..."

"But I am more powerful than the finger of a king," said the snake.

The little prince smiled. "You are not very powerful. You haven't even any feet. You cannot even travel..."

"I can carry you farther than any ship could take you," said the snake. He twined himself around the little prince's ankle, like a golden bracelet. "Whomever I touch, I send back to the earth from whence he came," the snake spoke again.

"But you are innocent and true, and you come from a star..." The little prince made no reply. "You move me to pity—you are so weak on this Earth made of granite," the snake said. "I can help you, someday, if you grow too homesick for your own planet. I can—"

"Oh! I understand you very well," said the little prince. "But why do you always speak in riddles?"

"I solve them all," said the snake. And they were both silent.

Chapter 18

The little prince crossed the desert and met with only one flower. It was a flower with three petals, a flower of no account at all.

"Good morning," said the little prince.

"Good morning," said the flower.

"Where are the men?" the little prince asked, politely.

The flower had once seen a caravan passing. "Men?" she echoed. "I think there are six or seven of them in existence. I saw them several years ago. But one never knows where to find them. The wind blows them away. They have no roots, and that makes their life very difficult."

"Goodbye," said the little prince.

"Goodbye," said the flower.

Chapter 19

After that, the little prince climbed a high mountain. The only mountains he had ever known were the three volcanoes, which came up to his knees. And he used the extinct volcano as a footstool. "From a mountain as high as this one," he said to himself, "I shall be able to see the whole planet at one glance, and all the people..." But he saw nothing, save peaks of rock that were sharpened like needles.

"Good morning," he said courteously.

"Good morning-Good morning-Good morning," answered the echo.

"Who are you?" said the little prince.

"Who are you—Who are you—Who are you?" answered the echo.

"Be my friends. I am all alone," he said.

"I am all alone—all alone-all alone," answered the echo.

"What a queer planet!" he thought. "It is altogether dry, and altogether pointed, and altogether harsh and forbidding. And the people have no imagination. They repeat whatever one says to them... On my planet I had a flower; she always was the first to speak..."

Chapter 20

But it happened that after walking for a long time through sand, and rocks, and snow, the little prince at last came upon a road. And all roads lead to the abodes of men.

"Good morning," he said. He was standing before a garden, all a-bloom with roses.

"Good morning," said the roses.

The little prince gazed at them. They all looked like his flower.

"Who are you?" he demanded, thunderstruck.

"We are roses," the roses said. And he was overcome with sadness. His flower had told him that she was the only one of her kind in all the universe. And here were five thousand of them, all alike, in one single garden!

"She would be very much annoyed," he said to himself, "if she should see that... She would cough most dreadfully, and she would pretend that she was dying, to avoid being laughed at. And I should be obliged to pretend that I was nursing her back to life—for if I did not do that, to humble myself also, she would really allow herself to die..."

Then he went on with his reflections: "I thought that I was rich, with a flower that was unique in all the world; and all I had was a common rose. A common rose, and three volcanoes that come up to my knees— and one of them perhaps extinct forever... That doesn't make me a very great prince..." And he lay down in the grass and cried.

Chapter 21

It was then that the fox appeared. "Good morning," said the fox.

"Good morning," the little prince responded politely, although when he turned around, he saw nothing.

"I am right here," the voice said, "under the apple tree."

"Who are you?" asked the little prince and added, "You are very pretty to look at."

"I am a fox," the fox said.

And he lay down in the grass and cried.

"Come and play with me," proposed the little prince. "I am so unhappy."

"I cannot play with you," the fox said. "I am not tamed."

"Ah! Please excuse me," said the little prince. But, after some thought, he added: "What does that mean—'tame'?"

"You do not live here," said the fox. "What is it that you are looking for?"

"I am looking for men," said the little prince. "What does that mean —'tame'?"

"Men," said the fox. "They have guns, and they hunt. It is very disturbing. They also raise chickens. These are their only interests."

"Are you looking for chickens?"

"No," said the little prince. "I am looking for friends. What does that mean 'tame'?"

"It is an act too often neglected," said the fox. It means to establish ties."

"To establish ties'?"

"Just that," said the fox.

"To me, you are still nothing more than a little boy who is just like a hundred thousand other little boys. And I have no need of you. And you, on your part, have no need of me. To you,

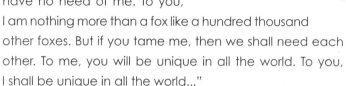

I am nothing more than a fox like a hundred thousand other foxes. But if you tame me, then we shall need each other. To me, you will be unique in all the world. To you, I shall be unique in all the world..."

"I am beginning to understand," said the little prince. "There is a flower... I think that she has tamed me...

"It is possible," said the fox. "On the Earth, one sees all sorts of things."

"Oh, but this is not on the Earth!" said the little prince.

The fox seemed perplexed and very curious. "On another planet?"

"Yes."

"Are there hunters on that planet?"

"No."

"Ah, that is interesting! Are there chickens?"

"No."

"Nothing is perfect," sighed the fox.

But he came back to his idea. "My life is very monotonous," the fox said. "I hunt chickens; men hunt me. All the chickens are just alike, and all the men are just alike. And, in consequence, I am a little bored."

"But if you tame me, it will be as if the sun came to shine on my life. I shall know the sound of a step that will be different from all the others. Other steps send me hurrying back underneath the ground. Yours will call me, like music, out of my burrow."

"And then look: you see the grain-fields down yonder? I do not eat bread. Wheat is of no use to me. The wheat fields have nothing to say to me. And that is sad. But you have hair that is the color of gold. Think how wonderful that will be when you have tamed me! The grain, which is also golden, will bring me back the thought of you. And I shall love to listen to the wind in the wheat..."

The fox gazed at the little prince for a long time. "Please— tame me!" he said.

"I want to, very much," the little prince replied. "But I have not much time. I have friends to discover, and a great many things to understand."

"One only understands the things that one tames," said the fox. "Men have no more time to understand anything. They buy things all ready made at the shops. But there is no shop anywhere where one can buy friendship, and so men have no friends any more. If you want a friend, tame me..."

"What must I do, to tame you?" asked the little prince.

"You must be very patient," replied the fox. "First, you will sit down at a little distance from me—like that— in the

"For example, if you come at four o'clock in the afternoon,then at three o'clock I shall begin to be happy.

grass. I shall look at you out of the corner of my eye, and you will say nothing. Words are the source of misunderstandings. But you will sit a little closer to me, every day..."

The next day the little prince came back. "It would have been better to come back at the same hour," said the fox. "If, for example, you come at four o'clock in the afternoon, then at three o'clock I shall begin to be happy. I shall feel happier and happier as the hour advances. At four o'clock, I shall already be worrying and jumping about. I shall show you how happy I am! But if you come at just any time, I shall never know at what hour my heart is to be ready to greet you..."

"One must observe the proper rites..."
"What is a rite?" asked the little prince.
"Those also are actions too often neglected," said the fox. "They are what make one day different from other days, one hour from other hours."

"There is a rite, for example, among my hunters. Every Thursday they dance with the village girls. So Thursday is a wonderful day for me! I can take a walk as far as the vineyards. But if the hunters danced at just any time, every day would be like every other day, and I should never have any vacation at all."

So the little prince tamed the fox. And when the hour of his departure drew near-"Ah," said the fox, "I shall cry."
"It is your own fault," said the little prince. "I never wished you any sort of harm; but you wanted me to tame you..."
"Yes, that is so," said the fox.
"But now you are going to cry!" said the little prince.
"Yes, that is so," said the fox.

"Then it has done you no good at all!"
"It has done me good," said the fox, "because of the color of the wheat fields." And then he added: "Go and look again at the roses. You will understand now that yours is unique in all the world. Then come back to say goodbye

to me, and I will make you a present of a secret."

The little prince went away, to look again at the roses. "You are not at all like my rose," he said. "As yet, you are nothing. No one has tamed you, and you have tamed no one. You are like my fox when I first knew him. He was only a fox like a hundred thousand other foxes. But I have made him my friend, and now he is unique in all the world." And the roses were very much embarrassed.

"You are beautiful, but you are empty," he went on. "One could not die for you. To be sure, an ordinary passerby would think that my rose looked just like you— the rose that belongs to me. But in herself alone she is more important than all the hundreds of you other roses: because it is she that I have watered; because it is she that I have put under the glass globe; because it is she that I have sheltered behind the screen; because it is for her that I have killed the caterpillars (except the two or three that we saved to become butterflies); because it is she that I have listened to, when she grumbled, or boasted, or ever sometimes when she said nothing. Because she is my rose.

And he went back to meet the fox. "Goodbye," he said.
"Goodbye," said the fox. "And now here is my secret, a very simple secret: It is only with the heart that one can see rightly. What is essential is invisible to the eye."
"What is essential is invisible to the eye," the little prince

repeated so that he would be sure to remember.

"It is the time you have wasted for your rose that makes your rose so important."

"It is the time I have wasted for my rose—" said the little prince, so that he would be sure to remember.

"Men have forgotten this truth," said the fox. "But you must not forget it. You become responsible, forever, for what you have tamed. You are responsible for your rose..."

"I am responsible for my rose," the little prince repeated so that he would be sure to remember.

Chapter 22

"Good morning," said the little prince.

"Good morning," said the railway switchman.

"What do you do here?" the little prince asked.

"I sort out travelers, in bundles of a thousand," said the switchman. "I send off the trains that carry them: now to the right, now to the left."

And a brilliantly lighted express train shook the switchman's cabin as it rushed by with a roar like thunder.

"They are in a great hurry," said the little prince. "What are they looking for?"

"Not even the locomotive engineer knows that," said the switchman.

And a second brilliantly lighted express thundered by, in the opposite direction.

"Are they coming back already?" demanded the little prince.

"These are not the same ones," said the switchman. "It is an exchange."

"Were they not satisfied where they were?" asked the little prince.

"No one is ever satisfied where he is," said the switchman.

And they heard the roaring thunder of a third brilliantly lighted express.

"Are they pursuing the first travelers?" demanded the little prince.

"They are pursuing nothing at all," said the switchman. "They are asleep in there, or if they are not asleep they are yawning. Only the children are flattening their noses against the windowpanes."

"Only the children know what they are looking for," said the little prince. "They waste their time over a rag doll, and it becomes very important to them; and if anybody takes it away from them, they cry..."

"They are lucky," the switchman said.

Chapter 23

"Good morning," said the little prince.

"Good morning," said the merchant. This was a merchant who sold pills that had been invented to quench thirst. You need only swallow one pill a week, and you would feel no need of anything to drink.

"Why are you selling those?" asked the little prince.

"Because they save a tremendous amount of time," said the merchant. "Computations have been made by experts. With these pills, you save fifty-three minutes in every week."

"And what do I do with those fifty-three minutes?"

"Anything you like..."

"As for me," said the little prince to himself, "if I had fifty-three minutes to spend as I liked, I should walk at my leisure toward a spring of fresh water."

Chapter 24

It was now the eighth day since I had had my accident in the desert, and I had listened to the story of the merchant as I was drinking the last drop of my water supply.

"Ah," I said to the little prince, "these memories of yours are very charming, but I have not yet succeeded in repairing my plane; I have nothing more to drink; and I, too, should be very happy if I could walk at my leisure toward a spring of fresh water!"

"My friend the fox-" the little prince said to me.
"My dear little man, this is no longer a matter that has anything to do with the fox!"
"Why not?"
"Because I am about to die of thirst..."
He did not follow my reasoning, and he answered me:
"It is a good thing to have had a friend, even if one is about to die. I, for instance, am very glad to have had a fox as a friend..."

"He has no way of guessing the danger," I said to myself. "He has never been either hungry or thirsty. A little sunshine is all he needs..." But he looked at me steadily and replied to my thought:
"I am thirsty, too. Let us look for a well..."
I made a gesture of weariness. It is absurd to look for a well, at random, in the immensity of the desert. But nevertheless,

we started walking.

When we had trudged along for several hours, in silence, the darkness fell, and the stars began to come out. Thirst had made me a little feverish, and I looked at them as if I were in a dream. The little prince's last words came reeling back into my memory:

"Then you are thirsty, too?" I demanded. But he did not reply to my question. He merely said to me:

"Water may also be good for the heart..."
I did not understand this answer, but I said nothing. I knew very well that it was impossible to cross-examine him.

He was tired. He sat down. I sat down beside him. And, after a little silence, he spoke again:

"The stars are beautiful, because of a flower that cannot be seen."

I replied, "Yes, that is so." And, without saying anything more, I looked across the ridges of sand that were stretched out before us in the moonlight.

"The desert is beautiful," the little prince added.
And that was true. I have always loved the desert. One sits down on a desert sand dune, sees nothing, hears nothing. Yet through the silence something throbs, and gleams...

"What makes the desert beautiful," said the little prince, "is that somewhere it hides a well..."
I was astonished by a sudden understanding of that mysterious radiation of the sands. The desert is beautiful because there is water cannot see.

When I was a little boy, I lived in an old house, and legend told us that a treasure was buried there. To be sure, no one had ever known how to find it; perhaps no one had ever even looked for it. But it cast an enchantment over that house. My home was hiding a secret in the depths of its heart...

"Yes," I said to the little prince. "The house, the stars, the desert-what gives them their beauty is something that is invisible!"

"I am glad," he said, "that you agree with my fox."

As the little prince dropped off to sleep, I took him in my arms and set out walking once more. I felt deeply moved and stirred. It seemed to me that I was carrying a very fragile treasure. It seemed to me, even, that there was nothing more fragile on all Earth. In the moonlight, I looked at his pale forehead, his closed eyes, his locks of hair that trembled in the wind, and I said to myself:

"What I see here is nothing but a shell. What is most important is invisible..."

As his lips opened slightly with the suspicion of a half-smile, I said to myself, again:

"What moves me so deeply, about this little prince who is sleeping here, is his loyalty to a flower-the image of a rose that shines through his whole being like the flame of a lamp, even when he is asleep..." And I felt him to be more fragile still. I felt the need of protecting him as if he himself were a flame that might be extinguished by a little puff of wind... And, as I walked on so, I found the well, at daybreak.

Chapter 25

"Men," said the little prince, "set out on their way in express trains, but they do not know what they are looking for. Then they rush about, and get excited, and turn round and round..." And he added: "It is not worth the trouble..."

The well that we had come to was not like the wells of the Sahara. The wells of the Sahara are mere holes dug in the sand. This one was like a well in a village.

But there was no village here, and I thought I must be dreaming...

"It is strange," I said to the little prince. "Everything is ready for use: the pulley, the bucket, the rope..."
He laughed, touched the rope, and set the pulley to working. And the pulley moaned, like an old weathervane which the wind has long since forgotten.

"Do you hear?" said the little prince. "We have wakened the well, and it is singing..." I did not want him to tire himself with the rope.

"Leave it to me," I said. "It is too heavy for you."

I hoisted the bucket slowly to the edge of the well and set it there—happy, tired as I was, over my achievement. The song of the pulley was still in my ears, and I could see the sunlight shimmer in the still trembling water.

"I am thirsty for this water," said the little prince. "Give me some of it to drink..."

And I understood what he had been looking for. I raised the bucket to his lips. He drank, his eyes closed. It was as sweet as some special festival treat. This water was indeed a different thing from ordinary nourishment. Its sweetness was born of the walk under the stars, the song of the pulley, the effort of my arms. It was good for the heart, like a present. When I was a little boy, the lights of the Christmas tree, the music of the Midnight Mass, the tenderness of smiling faces, used to make up, so, the radiance of the gifts I received.

"The men where you live," said the little prince, "raise five thousand roses in the same garden-and they do not find in it what they are looking for."

"They do not find it," I replied.

"And yet what they are looking for could be found in one single rose, or in a little water."

"Yes, that is true," I said.

And the little prince added: "But the eyes are blind. One must look with the heart..."

I had drunk the water. I breathed easily. At sunrise, the sand is the color of honey. And that honey color was making me happy, too. What brought me, then, this sense of grief?

"You must keep your promise," said the little prince, softly, as he sat down beside me once more.

"What promise?"

"You know—a muzzle for my sheep... I am responsible for this flower..."

I took my rough drafts of drawings out of my pocket. The little prince looked them over, and laughed as he said:

"Your baobabs—they look a little like cabbages."

"Oh!" I had been so proud of my baobabs!

"Your fox—his ears look a little like horns; and they are

too long." And he laughed again.

"You are not fair, little prince," I said. "I don't know how to draw anything except boa constrictors from the outside and boa constrictors from the inside."

"Oh, that will be all right," he said, "children understand."

So then I made a pencil sketch of a muzzle. And as I gave it to him my heart was torn. "You have plans that I do not know about," I said.
But he did not answer me. He said to me, instead:

"You know—my descent to the earth... Tomorrow will be its anniversary."

Then, after a silence, he went on: "I came down very near here." And he flushed. And once again, without understanding why, I had a queer sense of sorrow.

One question, however, occurred to me:
"Then it was not by chance that on the morning when I first met you—a week ago—you were strolling along like that, all alone, a thousand miles from any inhabited region? You were on the your back to the place where you landed?" The little prince flushed again.

And I added, with some hesitancy:
"Perhaps it was because of the anniversary?" The little prince flushed once more. He never answered questions-but when one flushes does that not mean "Yes"?

"Ah," I said to him, "I am a little frightened-"

But he interrupted me. "Now you must work. You must return to your engine. I will be waiting for you here. Come back tomorrow evening..."

But I was not reassured. I remembered the fox. One runs the risk of weeping a little, if one lets himself be tamed...

Chapter 26

Beside the well there was the ruin of an old stone wall. When I came back from my work, the next evening, I saw from some distance away my little prince sitting on top of a wall, with his feet dangling.

And I heard him say:

"Then you don't remember. This is not the exact spot."
Another voice must have answered him, for he replied to it:

"Yes, yes! It is the right day, but this is not the place."

I continued my walk toward the wall. At no time did I see or hear anyone. The little prince, however, replied once again:

"—Exactly. You will see where my track begins, in the sand. You have nothing to do but wait for me there. I shall be there tonight."

I was only twenty meters from the wall, and I still saw nothing. After a silence, the little prince spoke again:

"You have good poison? You are sure that it will not make me suffer too long?" I stopped in my tracks, my heart torn asunder; but still I did not understand.

"Now go away," said the little prince. "I want to get down from the wall."

I dropped my eyes, then, to the foot of the wall—and

"Now, go away, I want to get down from the wall."

I leaped into the air. There before me, facing the little prince, was one of those yellow snakes that take just thirty seconds to bring your life to an end.

Even as I was digging into my pocket to get out my revolver, I made a running step back. But, at the noise I made, the snake let himself flow easily across the sand like the dying spray of a fountain, and, in no apparent hurry, disappeared, with a light metallic sound, among the stones.

I reached the wall just in time to catch my little man in

my arms; his face was white as snow.

"What does this mean?" I demanded. "Why are you talking with snakes?" I had loosened the golden muffler that he always wore. I had moistened his temples and had given him some water to drink.

And now I did not dare ask him any more questions. He looked at me very gravely and put his arms around my neck. I felt his heart beating like the heart of a dying bird, shot with someone's rifle...

"I am glad that you have found what was the matter with your engine," he said. "Now you can go back home—"

"How do you know about that?" I was just coming to tell him that my work had been successful, beyond anything that I had dared to hope. He made no answer to my question, but he added:

"I, too, am going back home today..."

Then, sadly— "It is much farther... It is much more difficult..." I realized clearly that something extraordinary was happening. I was holding him close in my arms as if he were a little child; and yet it seemed to me that he was rushing headlong toward an abyss from which I could do nothing to restrain him...

His look was very serious, like someone lost far away.

"I have your sheep. And I have the sheep's box. And I have the muzzle..." And he gave me a sad smile. I waited a long time. I could see that he was reviving little by little.

"Dear little man," I said to him, "you are afraid..." He was afraid, there was no doubt about that. But he laughed lightly.

"I shall be much more afraid this evening..."
Once again I felt myself frozen by the sense of something irreparable. And I knew that I could not bear the thought of never hearing that laughter any more. For me, it was like a spring of fresh water in the desert.

"Little man," I said, "I want to hear you laugh again." But he said to me:

"Tonight, it will be a year... My star, then, can be found right above the place where I came to the Earth, a year ago..."

"Little man," I said, "tell me that it is only a bad dream—this affair of the snake, and the meeting-place, and the star..." But he did not answer my plea. He said to me, instead:

"The thing that is important is the thing that is not seen..."
"Yes, I know..."

"It is just as it is with the flower. If you love a flower that lives on a star, it is sweet to look at the sky at night. All the stars are a-bloom with flowers..."
"Yes, I know..."

"It is just as it is with the water. Because of the pulley, and the rope, what you gave me to drink was like music. You remember—how good it was."

"Yes, I know..."

"And at night you will look up at the stars. Where I live everything is so small that I cannot show you where my star is to be found. It is better, like that. My star will just be one of the stars, for you. And so you will love to watch all the stars in the heavens... they will all be your friends. And, besides, I am going to make you a present..."

He laughed again.

"Ah, little prince, dear little prince! I love to hear that laughter!"

"That is my present. Just that. It will be as it was when we drank the water..."

"What are you trying to say?"

"All men have the stars," he answered, "but they are not the same things for different people. For some, who are travelers, the stars are guides. For others they are no more than little lights in the sky. For others, who are scholars, they are problems. For my businessman, they were wealth.

But all these stars are silent. You—you alone-will have the stars as no one else has them-"

"What are you trying to say?"

"In one of the stars I shall be living. In one of them I shall be laughing. And so it will be as if all the stars were laughing when you look at the sky at night... You-only you-will have stars that can laugh!"

And he laughed again. "And when your sorrow is comforted (time soothes all sorrows) you will be content that you have known me. You will always be my friend. You will want to laugh with me. And you will sometimes open your window, so, for that pleasure... And your friends will be properly astonished to see you laughing as you look up at the sky! Then you will say to them, Yes, the stars always make me laugh!' And they will think you are crazy. It will be a very shabby trick that I shall have played on you..."
And he laughed again. "It will be as if, in place of the stars, I had given you a great number of little bells that knew how to laugh..." And he laughed again.

Then he quickly became serious:
"Tonight—you know... Do not come."
"I shall not leave you," I said.
"I shall look as if I were suffering. I shall look a little as if I were dying. It is like that. Do not come to see that. It is not worth the trouble..."
"I shall not leave you."

But he was worried. "I tell you—it is also because of the snake. He must not bite you. Snakes— they are malicious creatures. This one might bite you just for fun..."
"I shall not leave you." But a thought came to reassure

him:

"It is true that they have no more poison for a second bite."

That night I did not see him set out on his way. He got away from me without making a sound. When I succeeded in catching up with him he was walking along with a quick and resolute step. He said to me merely:

"Ah! You are there..."

And he took me by the hand. But he was still worrying.
"It was wrong of you to come. You will suffer. I shall look as if I were dead; and that will not be true..."
I said nothing.

"You understand... it is too far. I cannot carry this body with me. It is too heavy."
I said nothing.

And he sat down because he was afraid.

"But it will be like an old abandoned shell. There is nothing sad about old shells..."

I said nothing.

He was a little discouraged. But he made one more effort:

"You know, it will be very nice. I, too, shall look at the stars. All the stars will be wells with a rusty pulley. All the stars will pour out fresh water for me to drink..."

I said nothing.

"That will be so amusing! You will have five hundred million little bells, and I shall have five hundred million springs of fresh water..." And he too said nothing more, because he was crying...

He fell as gently as a tree falls.

"Here it is. Let me go on by myself." And he sat down because he was afraid. Then he said, again:

"You know, my flower... I am responsible for her. And she is so weak! She is so naive! She has four thorns, of no use at all, to protect herself against all the world..."

I too sat down, because I was not able to stand up any longer.

"There now-that is all..." He still hesitated a little; then he got up. He took one step. I could not move. There was nothing but a flash of yellow close to his ankle. He remained motionless for an instant. He did not cry out. He fell as gently as a tree falls. There was not even any sound, because of the sand.

Chapter 27

And now six years have already gone by... I have never yet told this story. The companions who met me on my return were well content to see me alive. I was sad, but I told them:

"I am tired."

Now my sorrow is comforted a little. That is to say-not entirely. But I know that he did go back to his planet because I did not find his body at daybreak. It was not such a heavy body... and at night I love to listen to the stars. It is like five hundred million little bells...

But there is one extraordinary thing... when I drew the muzzle for the little prince, I forgot to add the leather strap to it. He will never have been able to fasten it on his sheep. So now I keep wondering: what is happening on his planet? Perhaps the sheep has eaten the flower...

At one time I say to myself:

"Surely not! The little prince shuts his flower under her glass globe every night, and he watches over his sheep very carefully..." Then I am happy. And there is sweetness in the laughter of all the stars. But at another time I say to myself: "At some moment or other one is absent-minded, and that is enough! On some one evening he forgot the glass globe, or the sheep got out, without making any noise, in the night..." And then the little bells are changed to tears...

Here, then, is a great mystery. For you who also love the little prince, and for me, nothing in the universe can be the same if somewhere, we do not know where, a sheep that we never saw has-yes or no?-eaten a rose... Look up at the sky. Ask yourselves: is it yes or no? Has the sheep eaten the flower? And you will see how everything changes... And no grown-up will ever understand that this is a matter of so much importance!

This is, to me, the loveliest and saddest landscape in the world. It is the same as that on the preceding page, but I have drawn it again to impress it on your memory. It is here that the little prince appeared on Earth, and disappeared.

Look at it carefully so that you will be sure to recognize it in case you travel someday to the African desert. And, if you should come upon this spot, please do not hurry on. Wait for a time, exactly under the star.

Then, if a little man appears who laughs, who has golden hair and who refuses to answer questions, you will know who he is. If this should happen, please comfort me. Send me word that he has come back.

여기까지 오신 여러분께 아낌없는 찬사를 보냅니다. "레벨 5까지 올라오시느라, 고생 많으셨습니다!" 자, 이제 내려갈 일만 남았습니다. 끝난 게 아니냐고요? 지금까지의 과정을 '등산'이라고 생각해 보시면 어떨까요? 하산까지 해봐야 이 여정이 진짜 끝이납니다.

We would like to congratulate everyone who made it this far. "Well done climbing up to the Level 5 book!" Now, it is time for you to go down. Did you think it was over? Try to think of the entire process as "climbing a mountain." Going down a mountain is a must to complete the journey.

『단계 영어』에서의 하산이란, 복잡하고 어려운 문장이 어떻게 간결하고 쉬운 문장으로 변하는지를 체감하는 것입니다. 단계를 내려가며 읽으면, 요약적 사고를 키우는 데 큰 도움이 됩니다. 레벨5부터 시작하실 필요는 없습니다. 레벨 4부터 천천히 내려가세요. 그렇다고 챕터까지 거꾸로 읽진 마시고, 레벨만 한 단계씩 내려가며 읽어 보세요.

Going down a mountain in 『5 Steps English Book』 would mean thinking about how complicated and difficult sentences are changed into simple ones. As you go down the levels, you will be able to enhance your summarizing skills. You do not have to start from Level 5. Go down slowly from Level 4. Do not read the chapters from the back. Begin going down by reading the books one by one, in the descending order of levels.

이렇게 진행하면, 여러분은 '어린 왕자'를 영어로 총 아홉 번 읽게 됩니다. 이정도면 세상에 무서울 게 없지 않을까요? '다윗과 골리앗'에 나오는 다윗이 바로 여러분이 되는 것이지요. 이제는 당당하게 '어린 왕자' 원문을 읽읍시다.

This way, you will be reading The Little Prince a total of nine times. There will now be nothing that can scare you, right? You will be the David of the David and Goliath. You can now read The Little Prince confidently in English.

혹시 이 책으로 학습하고 싶은 분들이 계시면, 다음의 방법을 추천합니다. '동일 챕터별 읽기'인데요. 읽기라기보다는 영어 학습에 더 가깝습니다. 레벨별로 같은 챕터를 읽으며, 어휘와 문장 구조를 공부하는 것입니다. 예를 들어, 레벨 1의 챕터 1을 읽고, 레벨 2의 챕터 1을 읽으시면 됩니다. 짧은 시간에 같은 내용을 레벨별로 읽기에, 단어와 문장의 변화를 비교해 볼 수 있습니다.

If you like to study English with these books, we recommend you do as follows. "Reading the same chapters for each level." It is closer to studying rather than reading. If you read the same chapters for each level, you will be studying vocabulary and sentence structures. For example, read Chapter 1 of Level 1, then read Chapter 1 of Level 2. In a short period, you will be reading books with the same content, and you can compare the changes in the words and sentences.

'어린 왕자' 다음에는 '노인과 바다'와 '동물 농장'이 나올 예정입니다. 앞으로 나올 두 종류의 책까지 원서로 모두 읽으면, 여러분은 일반 원서도 부담 없이 읽는 능력을 갖출 것입니다.

After "The Little Prince," we will be publishing a series of books for "The Old Man & The Sea" and "Animal Farm." If you finish reading the next two sets, you will gain skills in reading English books.

단계 영어는 세계문학책과 동화책을 중심으로 제작될 예정입니다.
신간에 대한 최신 정보는 카카오채널 @icanread에서 받으실 수 있습니다.
다음 책인 "단계 영어 노인과 바다"에서 만나 뵙겠습니다.

We plan to make 5 Steps English Books with international literary books and fairy tales. To update yourselves with the new sets, please follow our Kakao Channel, @icanread.
We hope to see you in our next set of books,
"5 Steps English : The Old Man & The Sea."